Islam: A Very Short Introduction

VERY SHORT INTRODUCTIONS are for anyone wanting a stimulating and accessible way into a new subject. They are written by experts, and have been translated into more than 45 different languages.

The series began in 1995, and now covers a wide variety of topics in every discipline. The VSI library now contains over 500 volumes—a Very Short Introduction to everything from Psychology and Philosophy of Science to American History and Relativity—and continues to grow in every subject area.

## Titles in the series include the following:

Malise Ruthven

# ISLAM

## A Very Short Introduction

OXFORD
UNIVERSITY PRESS

# OXFORD
UNIVERSITY PRESS

Great Clarendon Street, Oxford OX2 6DP

Oxford University Press is a department of the University of Oxford.
It furthers the University's objective of excellence in research, scholarship,
and education by publishing worldwide in

Oxford New York

Auckland Cape Town Dar es Salaam Hong Kong Karachi
Kuala Lumpur Madrid Melbourne Mexico City Nairobi
New Delhi Shanghai Taipei Toronto

With offices in

Argentina Austria Brazil Chile Czech Republic France Greece
Guatemala Hungary Italy Japan Poland Portugal Singapore
South Korea Switzerland Thailand Turkey Ukraine Vietnam

Oxford is a registered trade mark of Oxford University Press
in the UK and in certain other countries

Published in the United States
by Oxford University Press Inc., New York

© Malise Ruthven 2012

The moral rights of the author have been asserted
Database right Oxford University Press (maker)

© First published as an Oxford University Press paperback 1997
Reissued 2000
This edition published 2012

British Library Cataloguing in Publication Data
Data available

Library of Congress Cataloging in Publication Data
Data available

Typeset by SPI Publisher Services, Pondicherry, India
Printed and bound by
CPI Group (UK) Ltd, Croydon, CR0 4YY
ISBN: 978–0–19–9642878

# Contents

# Preface to the second edition

Since 11 September 2001, the subject of Islam has come to the foreground of attention in the world's media. Words from the Islamic lexicon, like *jihad* (struggle, or 'holy war') and *fatwa* (legal ruling), as well as *hijab* (the head-covering worn by Muslim women), or *niqab* and *burqa* (the complete veils covering the female body), have entered the general vocabulary, as issues ranging from suicide bombings to female attire have entered the political and cultural consciousness of both Muslim majority countries and countries where Muslims form substantial minorities.

In this little book, I have tried to address some of the complexities surrounding recent controversies and events. To write a *Very Short Introduction* to the religion of approximately one-fifth of humanity at the present time has been a daunting assignment. Brevity depends on selection, and selection means exclusion. Given the vast diversity of human societies ranged under the label 'Islamic', any process of selection or exclusion must entail an element of distortion. In choosing to focus on some topics at the expense of others, I am conscious of following my own instincts and prejudices. Professionally, I have worked both as a journalist and academic, and have drawn on both disciplines. The journalist in me has an eye for the headlines. Aware that 'Islam' or 'Islamism' are seen as hostile forces by many people living in the West, as the main ideological challenge to post-Enlightenment liberalism since the Soviet collapse, I have given more space to politics than some would say the subject warrants. The same might be said of my chapter on women and the family – a controversial subject that looms large in today's media. At the same time, the scholar in me has tried to avoid the stereotyping or facile generalizations that usually accompany the treatment of these controversial subjects in the media.

Early drafts of the first edition of this book were read by my former and sadly missed colleague at Aberdeen University, the late Professor James Thrower, and the academic readers originally consulted by Oxford University Press. My thanks to them for suggestions for improvements, and to Deniz Kandiyoti who read an early draft of Chapter 5, and lent valuable insights from her rich reservoir of knowledge about Middle East cultures and feminism. This new edition owes much to discussions with friends and colleagues too numerous to name comprehensively. However, I would like to offer special thanks to George Miller, an exception-ally thoughtful and helpful editor who commissioned and guided the first edition; to the authors of numerous books included in the new, revised, reading list; and to the review editors – most notably Robert Silvers of the *New York Review of Books* – who granted me the privilege of reviewing them.

# List of Illustrations

The Publisher and the author apologize for any errors or omissions in the above list. If contacted they will be happy to rectify these at the earliest opportunity.

Islam

# List of maps

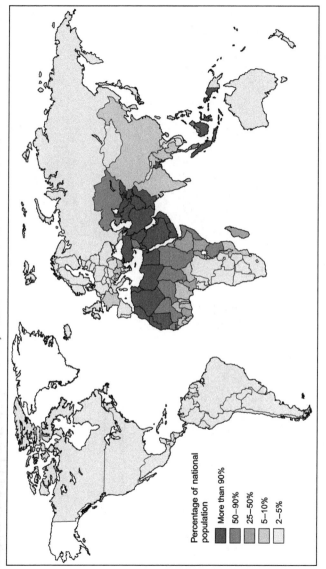

**Map 1. Muslims in the World**

Percentage of national population

- More than 90%
- 50–90%
- 25–50%
- 5–10%
- 2–5%

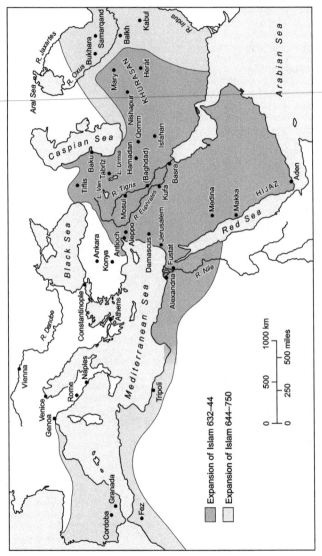

**Map 2. The Rise and Spread of Islam**

Expansion of Islam 632–44
Expansion of Islam 644–750

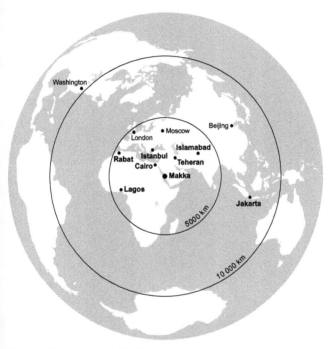

**Map 3. A Makka-centric World**

# Chapter 1
# Islam, Muslims, and Islamism

Since 11 September 2001, not a single day passes without stories about Islam – the religion of about one-fifth of humanity – appearing in the media. The terrorists who hijacked four American airliners and drove them into the World Trade Center in New York and the Pentagon near Washington, killing nearly three thousand people, not only served to trigger a 'war on terror' by the United States and its allies, leading directly to the removal of Muslim governments in Afghanistan and Iraq; it raised the profile of Islam throughout the world as a subject for analysis and discussion.

The debates, in newspaper columns and broadcasting studios, in cafés, bars, and homes, have been heated and passionate. Questions that were previously discussed in the rarefied atmosphere of academic conferences or graduate seminars have entered the mainstream of public consciousness. What is the 'law of jihad'? How is it that the 'religion of peace' subscribed to by millions of ordinary, decent believers seems to have become an ideology of hatred for an angry minority? Such questions are no longer 'academic', but are arguably of vital concern to most of the people living on this planet. That Islam, or some variation thereof – whether distorted, perverted, corrupted, or hijacked by extremists – has become a force to be reckoned with, or at least a label attached to a phenomenon with menacing potentialities, few would deny. Yet Muslims living in the West and in the growing areas of the Muslim world that come within the West's electronic footprint understandably resent the exposure that comes with the increasing concerns of outsiders. *Islam*, they would argue, is a religion of peace: the word Islam, a verbal noun meaning submission (to God), is etymologically related to the word *salam*, meaning peace. The standard greeting most Muslims use when joining a gathering or meeting strangers is *as-salaam ʿalaikum* – 'peace be upon you'. According to a widely held view, people who accuse Islam of being a violent religion misunderstand its essentially pacific nature.

Historically speaking, the balance of truth supports this view. In its earliest phase (up to around 750 CE), Islam was born on the wings of the Arab conquest, but in subsequent centuries its spread was largely peaceful, along a vast network of trade routes stretching from southern Africa to China and the South-East Asian archipelago and into the mountain valleys and steppelands of Central Asia. As a 'Religion of the Book', Islam carried with it the prestige of the high culture associated with great cities such as Cairo, Baghdad, and Delhi. Lacking a papacy or formal system for doctrinal and ritual enforcement, it proved especially adept at absorbing local traditions and customs derived from older religious traditions. In some cases, these were highly articulated religious systems, such as Zoroastrianism, Buddhism, or Hinduism; in others, they were shamanistic and animistic cults such as those found almost everywhere. The principal agents for spreading Islam in the peripheral regions were scholars and holy men (and sometimes women) who often doubled as merchants, and who proved adept at 'Islamizing' local cults and customs. Indeed, as scholars have noted, the use of the term 'conversion', with its presumption of conscious intentionality and individual choice, is inappropriate when dealing with the much more fluid processes of acculturation that occurred over the course of more than a millennium, when Islam became the world's second largest religion after Christianity. Orthodoxy – or to be more precise, orthopraxy, correct ritual practice or

behaviour in accordance with the central teachings of Islam –
sometimes followed, but not invariably, as people on the
periphery attained different levels of contact with Makka and the
urban centres.

Although Islamic rhetoric, harking back to the Prophet
Muhammad's campaigns in Arabia, was often invoked in the
course of military conflicts involving Muslims, the image of
perpetual or inherent militancy distorts the actual record of a
religion and civilization stretching back fifteen centuries over vast
expanses of territory from the shores of the Atlantic Ocean to the
Indonesian archipelago. The notion that Islam is inherently
violent is largely the result of two factors: recent colonial history
and the exaggerating effect of the media. From the 18th century,
when most of the Muslim world came under direct or indirect
Western control as a consequence of Europe's economic, military,
and industrial might, resistance to colonialism was spearheaded
by Muslim movements such as that of 'Abd al-Qadir against the
French in North Africa, the Sudanese Mahdi against the British in
the Sudan, and the Imam Shamil against the Russians in the
Caucasus. The image of cruelty and fanaticism (replicating some
of the themes that arose many centuries previously during the
Crusades) was forged at a time when European powers were in
conflict with Muslims who were defending their territories against
imperial encroachments.

More recently, this image has been compounded by the modern
media effect. In an age of sound-bites and newspaper agendas
driven by tabloid headlines, the lives and values of peace-loving
majorities are inevitably obscured by the attention-seeking acts of
the noisy minorities. The news media act like a distorting mirror
at a fairground, exaggerating the militancy of the few while
minimizing the quietism or indifference of the many. This
outstanding feature of modern societies has been successfully
exploited by extremists to draw attention to grievances and
minority political agendas. Terrorist acts, such as 9/11 or the

suicide bombings on London's public transport system that killed 52 innocent commuters in July 2005 and injured hundreds more, are not just meaningless acts of cruelty. They galvanize public attention by the 'propaganda of the deed', a tactic formulated by European anarchists in the 19th century. The responses of government may paradoxically build support for extremists by targeting whole communities or launching wars that challenge the loyalties of recently established citizens. In the globalized theatre dominated by media, events interact asymmetrically, creating unpredictable oscillations.

The Islamist attack on America, organized and facilitated by the Islamist al-Qaeda group under the leadership of Osama bin Laden, was largely inspired by the presence of US troops on the sacred soil of Saudi Arabia. This was itself a response to the threat to US oil supplies posed by the Iraqi leader Saddam Hussein's 1991 invasion of Kuwait. 9/11 and the logic of George W. Bush's 'war on terror' resulted in US-led wars against the Taliban regime in Afghanistan and the Saddam regime in Iraq. In due course, 7/7, as the London bombings came to be known, was motivated by anger on the part of a small group of young British-born Muslims at British participation in military campaigns against two Muslim-majority states, in which thousands of Muslims lost their lives. Fuelled by these unstable interactions, the prophecies of influential commentators such as Bernard Lewis of Princeton and the late Samuel Huntington of Harvard that a 'clash of civilizations' was looming between Islam and the West, appeared dangerously self-fulfilling. As the late Fred Halliday, a perceptive observer of international affairs, put it:

> The myth of confrontation is sustained from two apparently contradictory sides – from the camp of those, mainly in the West, seeking to turn the Muslim world into another enemy, and from those within the Islamic countries who advocate confrontation with the non-Muslim, particularly Western, world.

A horrifying demonstration of this logic occurred with the atrocities committed in July 2011 by right-wing extremist and self-confessed killer, Anders Behring Breivik, who massacred 69 people, most of them teenagers, on the island of Utøya, near Oslo, after killing 8 people with a car bomb in the Norwegian capital. The 1,500-page manifesto he posted on the internet shortly before his murderous rampage contained lengthy citations from British and American commentators who regard Islam as being fundamentally hostile to the West and the presence of Muslims in Europe as a threat to its Christian values and culture. As the Norwegian scholar Thomas Hegghammer has noted, Breivik's tract departs from established nostrums of the extreme right, such as white supremacism or ultra-nationalism, for a doctrine of 'civilizational conflict' that may represent the 'closest thing yet to a Christian version of al-Qaeda'. Both Breivik and the leaders of al-Qaeda see themselves as engaged in a conflict that extends back to the Crusades, with both using references to medieval chivalry. Both have resorted to catastrophic violence on behalf of transnational entities: the *umma*, or 'community', of all Muslims in the case of al-Qaeda, and 'Europe' in the case of Breivik. Both frame their struggles as wars of survival, with the emphasis placed on defending a religiously based culture rather than a distinctive nationality or ethnicity. Both hate their respective governments for 'collaborating' with the outside enemy. Both use the language of martyrdom. Where Islamists refer to suicide bombings as 'martyrdom operations', Breivik referred to an individual 'martyr cell' in anticipation of his attack on defenceless youngsters. Both, as Hegghammer notes, lament the erosion of patriarchy and the emancipation of women.

Breivik directed his rage, not at Muslims, but a youth camp of social democrats whom he saw as being likely to provide his country's future leadership and commitment to the Muslim-friendly, multiculturalist policies that he hated. Just as al-Qaeda represents an extreme, activist variant of political views held by a much wider constituency of Muslim radicals, most of whom would never consider crossing the boundary between thinking and action, Breivik (judging from his manifesto) holds a broad range of positions common to what might be called the 'counter-jihadist' or 'paranoid right'. All its supporters – most of whom denounced the Utøya massacre in the most unequivocal terms – subscribe to variants of the thesis that Europe is sleepwalking into cultural disaster or enabling Islamist terrorists to gain a dangerous foothold in its cities.

While the assassination of bin Laden by US special forces in May 2011, after a vastly expensive and lengthy intelligence operation, may have dealt a blow to his brand of extremism, it did nothing to resolve the underlying tensions between conflicting values and worldviews on which extremists rely for their support. The international al-Qaeda 'franchise' – which has spawned imitators or affiliates in numerous regions, including Somalia, Yemen, and the Maghreb – may have lost its iconic and titular head. But it was far from sure that the elimination of the man held responsible for the worst atrocity to have been committed on American soil was a strike for the 'war on terror' or a blow that would induce a further round of oscillations. Given the threat that the al-Qaeda leader posed to Muslim governments and people further afield, the responses were predictable. Along with the UN Secretary-General Ban Ki-moon, most governments – with the exception of Venezuela, Iran, and Syria – welcomed the elimination of the world's most wanted terrorist. But the execution of an unarmed man who had reportedly offered little, if any, resistance to his attackers, and the disposal of his body at sea (a questionable practice under Islamic law), amid scenes of public satisfaction in America, left many people, including the Archbishop of Canterbury, Dr Rowan Williams, with a 'very uncomfortable feeling' and infuriated radical groups who regarded bin Laden as their hero. In Egypt, the Muslim Brotherhood, leading beneficiaries of the fall of the Mubarak regime in February 2011, condemned the killing, calling it an 'assassination'; while its sister organization Hamas, which controlled the Gaza Strip in neighbouring Palestine, denounced the killing of an Arab *mujahid*, or 'holy warrior'. The Pakistani government, whose sovereignty had been violated in the attack on the compound near Islamabad where bin Laden had apparently been living for several years, vacillated between initially welcoming the Saudi dissident's death and condemning the 'unauthorized unilateral action' and 'unprovoked aggression' on the part of its nominal American ally. There were rallies in memory of bin Laden in several Pakistani cities, where American flags were burned, as well as in Sudan and in Turkey.

In death, as in life, bin Laden was a divisive figure. For the existing governments and the great majority of Muslims, he had perverted the Islamic message of justice, peace, and brotherhood by ordering terrorist acts that killed thousands of innocent people, many of them Muslims. For his admirers, he was an exemplary hero, living an austere and courageous life modelled ostensibly on that of the Prophet Muhammad, who had devoted a sizeable personal fortune to fighting Islam's enemies – principally the United States and its client regimes in the Muslim world 'in the path of Allah'. Bin Laden's life, and his death, raise some of the problematic questions to be addressed in the following pages.

Defining Islam is far from a simple matter. Using Western categories that may be alien to Muslim perceptions, we may state from the start that Islam may be both a religious faith and a political ideology; it is also, in some contexts, a mark of personal and group identity. These three definitions neither exclude nor include each other.

## Islam as identity

'Islam' in Arabic is a verbal noun, meaning self-surrender (to God) as revealed through the message and life of his Prophet, Muhammad. In its primary meaning (for example, as employed in the Quran and other foundational texts) the word 'Muslim' refers to one who so surrenders him- or herself (from the active participle of the verb *aslama*, to surrender oneself). There is, however, a secondary meaning to 'Muslim' which may shade into the first. A Muslim is one born to a Muslim father who takes on his or her parent's confessional identity without necessarily subscribing to the beliefs and practices of the faith, just as a Jew may define him- or herself as 'Jewish' without observing the Halacha. In non-Muslim societies, such Muslims may subscribe to, and be vested with, secular identities. The Muslims of Bosnia, descendants of Slavs who converted to Islam under Ottoman rule, have not always been noted for attendance at prayer, abstention from alcohol, seclusion of women, and other social practices associated with observant Muslims in other parts of the world. They were officially designated as Muslims to distinguish them from (Orthodox) Serbs and (Catholic) Croats under the former Yugoslavian communist regime. The label 'Muslim' indicates their ethnicity and group allegiance, but not necessarily their religious beliefs. In this limited context (which may also apply to other Muslim minorities in Europe and Asia), there may be no necessary contradiction between being Muslim and being atheist or agnostic, just as there are Jewish atheists and Jewish agnostics.

The word 'Christian', by contrast, has in normal usage come to imply a strictly confessional affiliation: a 'Christian atheist' – though occasionally employed by *avant-garde* theologians – sounds to most people like a contradiction in terms, although we can still speak of Western culture as predominantly Christian. It should be noted, however, that this secular definition of 'Muslim' (sometimes the terms 'cultural Muslim' or 'nominal Muslim' are used) is very far from being uncontested. Just as fundamentalist Christians in America have appropriated the term 'Christian' to apply exclusively to those who share their particular (usually narrow) versions of the faith, so modern Muslim activists have tended to redraw the boundaries between themselves and other Muslims who do not share their views, in extreme cases going so far as to designate the latter as 'infidels'. Generally, there is little

8

consistency in the way such labels are applied. Where Muslims, however secular or 'cultural', are beleaguered, as happened in Bosnia, a rhetorical generosity included them among the believers. Where, as in Egypt, a secular-minded majority may have opted to collaborate with a government perceived by its critics as too secular, such non-observant Muslims found themselves tarred with the 'infidel' brush. The words 'Islam' and 'Muslim' are disputed territory everywhere.

## Islam as political ideology

The word 'fundamentalist' is sometimes used to describe those Muslims who seek by whatever means to restore or establish an Islamic state. According to this view, it is the task of the Islamic state to enforce obedience to the revealed law of Islam – the Shari'a. The term 'fundamentalist' is problematic because of its Christian origins: fundamentalism was originally a movement directed against liberal or modernist theology as taught in American Protestant seminaries, in particular those teachings that questioned literal understandings of such supernatural events as six-day creation, the virgin birth, and the physical resurrection and imminent return of Christ. Many Muslim writers and ideologists described as 'fundamentalist' have adopted some modernistic and allegorical interpretations of the Quran, while virtually all believing Muslims – not just those described as 'fundamentalists' – see the Quran as the eternal unmediated Word of God. The focus for those seeking to defend Islam against what they see as the corrupting effects of modern secularism and the 'West' is *action* rather than *belief*. This agenda, however novel its methods of application (including the adoption of terrorist methods), generally accords with long-established historical patterns. Throughout history, Islamic rectitude has tended to be defined in relation to practice rather than doctrine. Muslims who dissented from the majority on issues of leadership or theology were usually tolerated provided their social behaviour conformed to generally accepted standards. It is in enforcing behavioural conformity (ortho*praxy*) rather than doctrinal conformity (ortho*doxy*) that Muslim radicals or activists look to a 'restoration' of Islamic law backed by the power of the state.

Before the popular demonstrations of the 'Arab Spring' of 2011 threw much of the Middle East into political turmoil, the means they adopted tended to vary. In some countries, such as Jordan, Muslim radicals sat as parliamentary representatives. In Egypt, though the Muslim Brotherhood was banned, members could sit as independents or members of other, allied parties. In Algeria as in Egypt under the former Mubarak regime, the more militant branches of the movement were engaged in an armed conflict with the state. In Sudan and formerly in Pakistan, Islamists have exercised power on the backs of military dictatorships. In Iran, they operate under a hybrid system, sitting as parliamentary representatives chosen from a restricted list of like-minded candidates. However, even when, as in Jordan, the democratic option may be adopted as a means to an end, democracy as such may be rejected. Most Muslims belonging to the militant tendency challenge the fundamentals of the international order: in the terms of one of their most influential mentors, Sayyid Abul Maududi (1903–79), they aim to replace the sovereignty of the people expressed through parliamentary legislation, with the 'sovereignty of God' as revealed, in its perfection and finality, through the Shari'a law.

Critics of this approach – and there are many – direct their fire at two of its arguments. Historically, they point out that no Islamic society, even during the high tide of Islamic civilization, was governed exclusively according to Islamic law. There was always a gap between the theoretical formulations of the jurists and the *de facto* exercise of political power. Moreover, given the enormous cultural and geographical differences between Muslim societies, Islamic law was everywhere supplemented by local customary laws. In legal-historical terms, the Shari'a was never an *overriding* reality.

The second, more damaging, criticism directed at those who insist on politicizing Islam, is misrepresentation. Far from being exclusively 'Islamic', the ideology or ideologies being advanced by the Islamists are really hybrids mixing Islamic concepts with 20th-century ideas, both liberal and totalitarian. The founders of modern political Islam – Abul Ala Maududi (1903–79), Sayyid Qutb (1906–66), and the Ayatollah Khomeini (1902–89) – were profoundly influenced by the Western political and intellectual cultures they professed to oppose. Thus Maududi's critique of Western materialism and moral decadence was informed by fascist attacks on democracy and an admiration for the dictators of the 1930s. Qutb's call for action against barbarism (*jahiliya*), far from being based on 'traditional' Islam, is thoroughly modern in its espousal of an 'existentialist', action-oriented commitment, while his claim that democracy and social justice have Islamic origins is considered by some to be spurious, based on an ahistorical reading of Islam's sacred texts. (Even the virulent anti-Semitism he adopted in the wake of the Arab–Israeli conflict is partly imported, influenced by European ideas.) Likewise, the 'Islamic' Constitution of Iran, introduced by Khomeini in 1979, is a mixture of Western and Islamic forms. It represents not so much an 'Islamic' constitution as an untrammelled assertion of the state's prerogatives based on the Jacobin model imported (without acknowledgement) from Europe. Far from being subject to Islamic law, Khomeini made it clear that the Islamic state, as successor to the Prophet Muhammad, had the power to override the Shari'a, even in such fundamentals of the faith as prayer, fasting, and pilgrimage.

In the view of political Islam's numerous critics, Muslim and non-Muslim, Islam as religion should be distinguished from Islam as political ideology. To call the latter 'fundamentalism' is not only misleading it makes a gratuitous concession to the advocates of political Islam by implying that the defence of Islam's 'fundamentals' invariably demands political action. Muslims who contest this view argue that so long as a government does not prevent the believer from carrying out his or her religious duties, it cannot be described as un- or anti-Islamic.

## Islam as faith

The classical authorities made a distinction between *islam* as professed by the Muslim on the one hand, and *iman*, or faith, of the *mumin* (believer) on the other. In the original wars that united the Arabian peninsula (see Chapter 2), the surrender or submission to God, however sincere, occurred through the exterior agencies of the Prophet and his followers. The American historian Fred Donner points out that many more of the Quran's messages are addressed to 'believers' than to 'muslims': the word 'believers' occurs almost a thousand times, compared with fewer than 75 instances of 'muslim'. The terms are not interchangeable: *islam* and *muslim* refer to submission or surrender, as in the case of the bedouin tribes who submitted to Muhammad in Arabia. 'Belief obviously means something different (and better) than "submission" (*islam*), and so we cannot simply equate the Believer with the Muslim, though some Muslims may qualify as Believers.'

The Quran alludes to an incident when a group of bedouin Arabs claim to have become believers and are told by God through the Prophet: 'You do not believe. Instead you may say: "we surrender," but faith has not entered your hearts.' (Quran 49: 14). Faith would follow surrender to the Muslim Prophet, conviction the appeal of his divine charisma. In due course, the degree of conviction required of the believer became the subject of theological debate. The puritanical Kharijis (Seceders) cast their net very narrowly, denying grave sinners the right to call themselves Muslims. The same puritanical tendency has been revived by militant groups today, who exclude lax or nominal Muslims from their definition of the *umma*, the worldwide community of believers. The Kharijis had a doctrine called listi'rad whereby they killed even the women and children of people they considered infidels. They can be seen as the original terrorists. The Kharijis' opponents, known as the Murjia, allowed that virtually anyone could be considered a Muslim so long as they proclaimed the *shahada*, the public declaration of faith enshrined in the formula 'There is no god but God; Muhammad is the Messenger of God'. Most of the classical authorities took the broader view. Abu Hanifa, whose name was given to one of the four legal schools of Sunni Islam, stated that 'those who face in the direction of Makka at prayer are true believers and no act of theirs can remove them from the faith'. In time, a majority of Muslims came to accept the view that *iman* and *islam* represented the internal and external aspects of religious commitment, faith and works. The exoteric or 'outward' manifestations of the faith, through observance of ritual and adherence to the Shari'a law, defined the Muslim *vis-à-vis* the outside world; but many came to consider that true piety was to be found in esoteric dimensions of the faith known only to a spiritual elite. In the absence of a formally constituted hierarchy or 'church', members of this elite were known by their knowledge of the religious disciplines and their command of spiritual or ascetical practices not normally acquired by the majority. Among the Shi'i minority, the spiritual elite is characterized by its proximity in kinship to the Prophet Muhammad and his family. Esotericism, including the exploration of hidden meanings in scripture and secret or unconventional religious practices, became the hallmark of movements that dissented from the majority politically or in religious style. The broadly tolerant view that determined Islam exoterically, by reference to *islam* as distinct from *iman*, allowed a great variety of spiritual growths to flourish without scandal. Although seekers after political power tended to wrap themselves in religious symbols just as avidly as they did in the West in pre-modern times, with polemicists routinely accusing each other of heresy, the history of Islam, however scarred by violence, is remarkably free from the forms of religious intolerance that found expression in the medieval and Spanish inquisitions. In modern times, the sense of inner commitment linking the believer to God in a personal relationship that may transcend the external imperatives of ritual and law has, despite appearances to the contrary, greatly assisted the privatization and secularization of the faith.

No religion could prosper and survive, as Islam has prospered and survived into modern times, if it were exclusively bound by the outward or exoteric forms of observance. No less than other successful modern religions, Islam contains a rich repertoire of concepts, symbols, and spiritual disciplines through which believers maintain their identities and sense of being in the world, their sense of being in contact with God. The crisis many Muslims are facing in adjusting to the realities of the contemporary world is not the result of some inherent lack of flexibility in the realm of ideas. Historically, Islam has shown enormous adaptability in accommodating different cultural systems within its overarching framework: the Abrahamic 'family' of western Asian monotheism that includes Judaism and Christianity as well as Islam.

The crisis of modern Islam – and few would deny that such a crisis exists – is not so much a 'spiritual crisis' as a crisis of authority – political, intellectual, and legal as well as spiritual. The 'best community' ordained by God for 'enjoining what is right and forbidding what is wrong' – a community that successfully conducted its own affairs for centuries, without external interference – demands leadership. Yet outside the Shi'i minority tradition, a leadership commanding universal support is conspicuously absent.

## Institutional leadership

There is no 'church' in Islam, no formally instituted body empowered to supervise or dictate the religious agenda, to articulate an 'official' Islamic view comparable to that of the Papacy or the appointed or elected leadership of Protestant denominations. With the collapse of the Islamic superstate that lasted barely two centuries after the death of the Prophet

Muhammad, religious authority was entrusted to the *'ulama* (sing.: *'alim*, 'learned man'), a class of scholars, whose role as guardians and interpreters of the tradition is much closer to that of the rabbis in Judaism than that of a Christian priesthood. They did not exercise political power but acted as a break on the power of the rulers, the *sultans* ('authorities') and *amirs* ('commanders'), most of whom came to power by force of arms, interpreting and administering the divine law according to complex rules developed in the academies. The most prestigious of these academies, Al-Azhar in Cairo, was founded in 971 CE and claims to be the oldest university in the world. Though its rector – the Shaikh al-Azhar – enjoys pre-eminence among the Sunni *'ulama*, his opinions are not binding on his peers; similarly, though all Muslim governments will appoint an official *mufti*, an *'alim* possessed of the authority to deliver legal judgements on a variety of issues, his opinions are purely consultative unless given effect in a court judgment by a *qadi*, a judge. It is the ruler who appoints the judge, so the implementation of the religious law, but not its interpretation, is under state control. Mass education policies undertaken by most post-colonial governments have led to a relative decline in the prestige and authority of the *'ulama* as graduates with mainly secular educational backgrounds forge their own interpretations of Islam's sacred texts, short-circuiting the traditional body of scholarship. Alternatively, in countries which have been less subject to modernizing influences, such as Afghanistan or the rural parts of Pakistan, *'ulama* or aspiring *'ulama* may seek to exercise power directly, oblivious of the modern world's complex realities. In either case, the crisis of intellectual authority is ultimately the same: the traditionally trained *'ulama* have failed to incorporate contemporary modernist or reformist thinking into their discourse. Activists seeking to 'Islamize' their societies, bringing them more closely into line with what they perceive to be Islamic law, ignore the centuries of nuanced and qualifying scholarship by which the *'ulama* in the past reconciled the demands of the divine law with the realities of political power and the exigencies of everyday life.

## Legal modernization

That there is a serious gap between the requirements of Islamic law and the actual legal practice of most Muslim majority states is arguably a matter of perception rather than reality. Earlier this century, a great modern jurist, 'Abd al-Razzaq Sanhuri, worked hard to reconcile Islamic law with the Western systems of law introduced under the colonial and post-colonial governments of Muslim states. Radical Muslims who demand that the Shari'a be 'restored' in its entirety are not acknowledging the extent to which this work, which was incorporated into the domestic legislation of many Muslim states, found common ground between formerly competing legal systems. In practice, demands for the 'restoration' of the Shari'a tend to focus on particular aspects of the criminal law, notably the corporal punishments specified in the Quran and early Muslim tradition for sexual offences and certain categories of theft. In some parts of the world, the *hudud* penalties (according to which transgressions of the 'limits' or 'boundaries' prescribed by God in the Quran are given specified punishments, such as amputation for theft or flogging for sexual relations outside marriage) have acquired a symbolic significance precisely because they are seen to confront licentious attitudes deemed to have been inspired by a 'decadent' West. Less controversially, the traditional Islamic ban on *riba*, understood as all forms of money loaned at interest, has led to some creative experiments in financial risk-sharing and equity participation by Islamic banks, which try to apportion the risks undertaken by lenders and borrowers more equitably than the conventional banking system does. Here, the Islamic concern for equity in business relationships offers a challenge to a post-Christian world afflicted by the recent banking crisis where corporate greed flourishes at the expense of the individual or family needs. Generally, however, demands for the 'restoration' of the Shari'a are part of what the late Algerian-born scholar Muhammad Arkoun called the 'social imaginary' of Muslims – the 'collection of images' held within a culture about itself or other cultures, images that tend to preclude analysis and objective self-reflection while feeding fantasies based on romantic, ahistorical visions of the past.

## Successes and failures of the Islamic state

The social imaginary, or better, perhaps social *memory*, lies at the heart of the collective aspirations which hark back to a golden age when *dar al-islam* (the sphere of Islam, distinguished in Islamic legal tradition from *dar al-harb*, the sphere of war) was still expanding and Muslim communities excelled in all the arts of civilization. No one need doubt that, at the level of civilization, an unprecedented degree of knowledge, excellence, and sophistication was achieved in *dar al-islam* several centuries before the Renaissance occurred in Europe, or that, as many scholars have noted, much of the groundwork for the scientific and philosophical thought that would flourish in the West was laid in Muslim lands. A short introductory text such as this can barely hint at the achievements of Muslims in the areas in which they excelled – architecture and design, metalwork and ceramics, poetry and philosophy, as well as the 'harder' sciences including mathematics, optics, astronomy, and medicine. Apart from the restrictions of space, however, there remains the thorny question of how far such cultural achievements are 'Islamic' in the sense that they can be attributed directly or even indirectly to the religion of Islam, and how far they built on and carried forward the achievements of preceding (mainly Greek and Persian) civilizations. The American historian Marshall Hodgson distinguished between 'Islamic' (pertaining to the religion) and 'Islamicate' (pertaining to the broader cultural and societal frame of which the religion is part, and over which it may be said to preside). The distinction is a useful one, even though it has not been widely adopted, and probably raises as many questions as it answers.

More central to the concerns of this essay are the problems of authority and power. Islamdom, like Christendom, its historical rival, aspires to universality. The failure of *dar al-islam* to maintain its initial momentum and to incorporate the globe within its domain hardly requires explanation, given the limitations of pre-modern technologies: the vastness of the territories encompassed by the Arabs in the first wave of invasions are astonishing enough in an era when the maximum distance a human being could travel (under the most favourable conditions) would have been no more than thirty or forty miles per day. The very speed and range of the initial expansion, however, were the source of political problems that remain unresolved after thirteen centuries. Islam initially expanded on the wings of tribalism. Submission to 'God and his Prophet' was, in the first instance, submission to a victorious bedouin army. From the first, the message of social justice and the equality of men (and, more problematically, of women) before God, as conveyed in Muhammad's preaching and preserved in the Quran, came up against the realities of tribal and dynastic power. The civil wars that occurred within a generation of the Prophet's death in 632, the split between Sunni and Shi'a, the collapse of the Arab empire, and the political fragmentation that occurred in its wake – all of these historical events bear witness to an unfulfilled project: the establishment of divine government on earth.

In the absence of church or priesthood, the execution of the project was left to the uncertainties of lay enthusiasts. Leadership was assumed by two elements, often in contradiction to each other. On one side, it passed to the tribal leaders for whom Islam (sometimes in its most heterodox, messianic versions) became the cement of tribal solidarity, the ideological force which directed energies previously consumed in internecine struggles outwards towards conquest; on the other, to the *'ulama*, the lay interpreters of the law, respected guardians of the tradition, but possessing no executive powers and reliant on outsiders, sometimes brought in as slaves from distant regions, to carry out God's commands. An uneasy compromise between these two agencies, the military rulers and the *'ulama*, produced a rough and ready constitutional balance in what has been called an 'international civilization', the first perhaps, in history. As Marshall Hodgson argued with passion and conviction, the 'Venture of Islam' did much to satisfy the needs of people in the urban regions lying between the Nile and Oxus rivers by facilitating the emergence of a common trading area based on the shared values of justice and fair dealings under God.

This historical achievement (which may without too much distortion appear as a golden age in the social memory of Muslims) was counter-balanced by a conspicuous failure at the level of power politics. After its initial expansion, the Arab empire imploded. Islam's central institution, the caliphate, at first contested by rival factions was gradually drained of legitimacy, as the caliph, the 'shadow of God on earth' became the prisoner of palace guards recruited from the tribes. The social memory focuses on several towering caliphal figures; the Four Rightly Guided Caliphs – Abu Bakr (r. 632–4), 'Umar (634–44), 'Uthman, and 'Ali (656–61); and the great Harun al-Rashid (786–809), the ideal monarch immortalized in the stories of the *Thousand and One Nights*, when the Arab empire was at its height. What social memory cannot address, of course, is the essential ambiguity of the caliphate. Scholars are still debating whether the early caliphate was a religious or political office, or a combination of both, and (if so), in what proportions. The term is as ambiguous as the office it describes. In the Quran, it is applied to Adam, the first man and God's vice-regent, and to David, a prophet who is also a king. The office as such emerged spontaneously after the death of the Prophet, who left no clear successor or rules for the succession. The first four caliphs succeeded by acclamation, in accordance with tribal custom. Some jurists argued that thereafter the true caliphate ceased, and that subsequent caliphs were merely monarchs or kings. In orthodox writings, the title 'caliph' generally means deputy or successor to the Prophet Muhammad (as in *khalifat rasul Allah* – deputy to the Messenger of God). Early Umayyad caliphs and some of the Abbasids who supplanted them employed the title *khalifat Allah* – deputy or vice-regent of God (as did some later Muslim sovereigns, such as the Sultan of Jogjakarta in Java). It seems clear that until the middle of the 9th century, the caliph exercised spiritual functions in addition to his political ones, enforcing religious conformity. After a populist reaction against efforts by the caliph al-Mamun to impose what are sometimes described as rationalist doctrines on government officials, through the *mihna*, or 'inquisition', the attempt at centralized control was abandoned, and guardianship of orthodoxy passed to the *'ulama*.

The consequences of the caliphal debacle are far-reaching when the destiny of Islamic governance is compared with that of Christianity in the West, where the Church retained a monopoly over Christian doctrine and the rituals that guaranteed salvation under vigorous Papal control. Although the Catholic monopoly was eventually broken, the Church's long hegemony effected social transformations that transcended the bonds of kinship. The occidental state merged as the Church – the ideal corporation embodying the person of Christ – gave birth to secular offspring in the shape of cities and other public entities. The Islamic state, by contrast, neverfully transcended its tribal matrix. The implosion of the Arab empire compounded the Caliph's failure to enforce religious conformity. Apart from the Shi'a, who held to the idea of a transcendent spiritual authority, the lack of any central institution in Islam charged with the task of religious governance paradoxically impeded the emergence of its counterweight in the shape of the secular state. The law developed separately from the agencies entrusted with its enforcement, and so military-tribal rule became the norm. As Patricia Crone and Martin Hinds have argued, 'a ruler who has no say at all in the definition of the law by which his subjects have chosen to live cannot rule those subjects in any but a purely military sense'. To perpetuate itself, such a state had to be manned by outsiders, and it is as outsiders, not as representatives of the community, that the rulers were obeyed. Although there was an element of consensus in this relationship, there was also, as Crone and Hinds point out, a total lack of institutional machinery behind [it]...The state was thus something which sat on top of society, not something which was rooted in it: and given that there was minimal interaction between the two, there was also minimal political development: dynasties came and went, but it was only the dynasties that changed.

This formulation may exaggerate the degree of political immobility in Muslim states, but it makes an important point about the relationship between the state and civil society in Muslim lands prior to the modern period (roughly from the 19th century), when Muslim rulers became aware of the need to introduce changes into their societies in order to face the military and economic challenges posed by the West.

## A religious awakening?

However much the experts may disagree on its long-term political implications, the resurgence of Islamic observance in daily life – increasing attendance at mosque, observance of fasting during Ramadan, a proliferation of religious publications in print and audio-visual media, and increasing emphasis on 'Islamic dress' in many parts of the world, especially for women – is undeniable. Two of the factors most frequently cited in explanation are the unprecedented scale of urbanization and the failure of the post-colonial state to deliver on its promises. Migration to the cities means both the loss of village life, where extended family networks reinforce traditional social values, and exposure to modern urban life, with its Westernized customs. On the political level, the collapse of communism and the failure of Marxism to overcome the stigma of 'atheism' makes Islam seem an attractive ideological weapon against post-colonial regimes perceived as corrupt and authoritarian and sometimes tyrannical. In countries lacking effective democratic institutions, the mosque and the network of activities surrounding it can enjoy a degree of immunity. If governments dare to close down 'rebel' mosques, they confirm the charges of disbelief levelled against them by their opponents.

The explosion of information technology, and particularly the revolution in audio-visual communication, undercuts the authority of the older literate elites, who tended to espouse secular values and lifestyles, while exposing ever-growing numbers of people to transgressive and often salacious images created by the Western entertainment and advertising industries. In many countries, an exponential leap in the rate of urbanization has decisively altered the cultural and demographic balance between urban and rural populations, creating a vast new proletariat of recently urbanized migrants susceptible to the messages of populist preachers and demagogues. In countries such as Egypt, the Islamist political movements, through their welfare organizations, have been able to fill the gaps caused by government failure to deal with poverty and housing shortages as well as other social problems caused by over-rapid urbanization. In recent years, these demographic trends have been overlaid by a new urban generation adept at using social media, giving rise to what is sometimes called the 'Facebook Revolution' in the Middle East. At the time of writing, the relationship between two social forces – the rural and recently urbanized who tend to adhere to traditional Islamic norms, and the generation of university and high-school graduates who are more inclined to identify with their Western peers – has yet to be tested. But in the absence of opposition structures rooted in civil society institutions, power may yet default to the armed forces, or to the Islamist movements with their networks of activists and organizational skills.

## Or a spiritual vacuum?

In pre-modern times, before the colonial period, Islamic societies were bound together not only by family and clan solidarities, but by the mystical Sufi brotherhoods to which most adult male members in urban societies belonged (see Chapter 4). Although the Islamic revival has been accompanied to some degree by a revival of Sufi practices, the combined impact of the post-colonial nationalist struggle and the modernist movement led to a drastic decline of Sufism, seen by modernizers as a mark of 'backwardness' and by religious purists as tainted by heresy or, even worse, by paganism. Yet in the absence of a priesthood, the Sufi *shaikhs* ('old men'), *murshids* (spiritual guides), or *pirs* (as they are known in Persian- and Urdu-speaking lands) were a source of spiritual authority that complemented and sometimes exceeded the intellectual authority of the *'ulama*. Though some Sufi brotherhoods took a leading part in the anti-colonial struggles, others collaborated with the colonial authorities. The latter saw them as allies against the modernists and reformers who pioneered the modern nationalist movements. Sufism, with its 'vision of union and oneness', its ascetical other-worldly orientation, and its concern with the esoteric dimensions of the faith, transcends the mundane particularities of politics, and the inevitably corrupting effects of power. Peter Von Sivers, an American scholar, links the rise of the modern political movements in Islam directly to the decline of Sufism, which many would see as the spiritual heart and soul of Islam. The exclusion of Sufism from the debate between secular-minded reformists and their religiously oriented opponents makes for an increasingly arid confrontation between violent extremes.

## Conclusion: Islam and Islamism

The religious revival in modern Islam is a reflection of the pace of social and technological change in the Muslim world, particularly the disruptive effects of a rapid increase in urbanization. In this respect, the causes are similar to those in Latin America and parts of sub-Saharan Africa where the late 20th century has seen a massive increase in the activities of Protestant churches. However, the increase in Islamic observance evidenced by such indicators as prayer, fasting, and attendance at the *Hajj*, the annual pilgrimage to Makka, is inevitably associated with the political aspirations of Muslims, most of whom live in post-colonial states run by governments perceived as lacking in moral or spiritual authority. The rise of mass education and, increasingly, the appearance of

1. The Ka'ba, the cube-shaped temple at the centre of the Noble Sanctuary in Makka. Pilgrims circumambulate the Ka'ba and Muslims everywhere pray in its direction. The *Kiswa*, or black silk covering, is replaced every year

**2. The Hajj terminal, King 'Abdul 'Aziz International Airport near Jedda, Saudi Arabia. The vast tented halls constructed from insulated fabrics developed in space research can accommodate pilgrims at the rate of 5,000 per hour, enhancing the accessibility and affordability of the *Hajj***

audio-visual modes of communication, has led to a decline in traditional sources of religious authority among both the *'ulama* and the leadership of the Sufi brotherhoods. Until recently, the gap has been filled by a variety of movements and leaders, most of whom claim a religious legitimacy for their acts. There are many historical precedents for movements of religious revival challenging and sometimes taking power in Islamic countries before the colonial and post-colonial international order brought most of the world into its economic and cultural orbit.

It would be wrong to conclude from this, however, that contemporary Islamic political movements are no more than the latest examples of an age-old cyclical pattern. The revivalist movements which often seem to dominate the headlines are modern, not just in their methods, which may include sophisticated techniques of organization as well as the use of guns, rockets, and bombs. They are modern in that they have absorbed into a 'traditional' Islamic discourse many ideas imported from outside the Islamic intellectual tradition. The decline in traditional forms of spirituality represented by the Sufi brotherhoods has been accompanied by the 'ideologization' of Islam at the political level, the construction of a political ideology using some symbols culled from the historical repertoire of Islam, to the exclusion of others. This ideology, sometimes referred to as 'Islamic fundamentalism', is better described as *Islamism*: the Latin suffix attached to the Arabic original reflects the usage of the Islamists themselves, who refer to themselves as *islamiyan* to distinguish themselves from the more general *muslimun* ('Muslims'). It more accurately expresses the relationship between the pre-existing reality (in this case, a religion) and its translation into a political ideology, just as communism ideologizes the reality of the commune, socialism the social, and fascism the ancient symbol of Roman consular authority. Islamism is not Islam. Though the lines dividing them are frequently blurred, it is important to distinguish between them.

# Chapter 2
# **The Quran and the Prophet**

Before the mid-20th century, Muslims were often referred to as Muhammadans, the religion of Islam as Muhammadanism. That the usage has been abandoned is partly a reflection of the political changes that have occurred since the time when most of the Islamic world was under European colonial rule. Europeans, especially in south Asia, saw the respect Muslims accord their Prophet as tantamount to worship. Muslims did not usually refer to themselves as Muhammadans (except as a descriptive term when addressing Europeans), because to do so would seem to imply that they worshipped Muhammad as Christians worshipped Christ. For orthodox Muslims such an implication was highly offensive. Muslims worship God, not Muhammad. The Messenger was a prophet, not a deity or divine avatar. To suggest otherwise would be to breach the boundary between God and humankind, the creator and his creation. Theologically maintenance of that boundary is the central article of the Islamic faith. 'There is no god but God. Muhammad is the Messenger of God.'

That is not to say that Muhammad is in any sense ordinary, or that his role is less central to the formation of Islam than Christ's is to that of Christianity. Arguably, the reverse applies. Because of the voluminous nature of the Islamic canon there are many more actions, thoughts, and sayings attributed to Muhammad than there are to Jesus. The difference lies not in his historical influence or the degree of fascination exercised over the minds of his followers, but rather in the different status accorded to his utterances. Muslims of all persuasions distinguish between those sayings attributed to Muhammad in his capacity as a prophet or divine revelator – utterances that are collected in the Quran (in its original meaning, the 'discourse' or 'recitation'); and those of a lesser status recorded by his contemporaries in a secondary body of scripture known as the *hadith* (reports or 'traditions'). Though some degree of controversy surrounds both categories, this difference of status is something on which Muslim and non-Muslim commentators are generally agreed.

## The Quran

For the vast majority of Muslims the Quran is the speech of God, dictated without human editing. It is more than a sacred text such as is found in other traditions. Following the Mu'tazili controversy (see pp. 58–9 below), the Quran came to be regarded as 'uncreated', hence co-extensive with God. As Wilfred Cantwell-Smith observes, it occupies for believing Muslims the position Christ has for Christians. A Muslim should not handle the text unless he or she is in a state of ritual purity. The exact pronunciation is as important as the meanings; unlike most Arabic texts, the Quranic script is supplied with the short vowel-sign to ensure the greatest degree of oral accuracy. Readings are preceded by the phrase 'I take refuge with God from Satan, the accursed one', and followed by 'God Almighty has spoken truly!' The opening and closing formulae establish 'a sort of verbal ritual enclosure or sanctuary around the recited text, preserving it from evil promptings or insincerity'. Certain verses are credited with curative powers: for example, the first *sura*, or chapter, known as the Opening, is good for scorpion bites; the last two (*suras* 113 and 114) are good for various illnesses.

Much scholarly argument surrounds the assemblage of the text. Most non-Muslim scholars, with a few exceptions, accept that the written book contains a record of the divine utterances made by Muhammad in the course of his prophetic ministry starting around 610 CE and ending with his death in 632. According to various traditions, Muhammad fell into a trance-like state when revelations came to him. These traditions are consistent with accounts of revelations received by more recent prophets, such as Joseph Smith Jr, the founder of Mormonism, whose prophetic utterances are contained in the scripture known as *Doctrine and Covenants*. Muslim historians are generally agreed that some or all of these utterances, which are carefully distinguished from Muhammad's 'normal' speech as recorded in the *hadith* literature, were written down during his lifetime. Each of the four 'Rightly Guided' Caliphs has been credited with initiating or forwarding the collection of the text. However, the historians and traditionists are unanimous that the official codex was adopted under the third Caliph 'Uthman (r. 644–56). Variant readings were eventually destroyed, but not entirely eliminated – a task made difficult by the condition of the earliest Arabic writing, which lacks the diacritical points used to distinguish consonants from each other. As the script evolved, so the text became standardized. The variant readings have been reduced to seven, each of which is regarded as equally valid.

The book is organized into 114 *suras* (literally 'rows'), or chapters, arranged approximately in order of length, with the shortest at the end and the longest near the beginning. The most important exception to this pattern is the first *sura*, the Fatiha, or Opening, a seven-verse invocation repeated during the five prayers Muslims are required to perform every twenty-four hours. Sometimes called the 'Mother of the Book', the Fatiha is seen as the quintessence of Islam. It is in frequent use as a prayer.

In the subsequent *suras*, the same fundamental message is repeated, elaborated, amplified, and illustrated with stories using the repertoire of Judaeo-Christian tradition with the addition of some distinctive Arabian elements. Adam and Noah, Abraham and

## The Opening

*'In the name of God,*
*Merciful to all,*
*Compassionate to each!*
*Praise be to God, Lord of the Worlds:*
*Merciful to all, Compassionate to each!*
*Lord of the Day of Judgement.*
*It is You we worship, and upon You we call for help.*
*Guide us to the straight path,*
*The path of those upon whom Your grace abounds,*
*Not those upon whom anger falls,*
*Nor those who are lost'.*
Quran 1: 1–7

## The Quran encapsulated

'[The Fatiha] contains, in a condensed form, all the fundamental principles laid down in the Quran: the principle of God's oneness and uniqueness, of his being the originator and fosterer of the universe, the fount of all life-giving grace, the One to whom man is ultimately responsible, the only power that can really guide and help, the call to righteous *action* in the life of this world, . . . the principle of life after death and of the organic consequences of man's action and behaviour, . . . the principle of guidance through God's message-bearers . . . and, flowing from it, the principle of continuity of all true religions . . . ; and finally, the need for voluntary self-surrender to the will of the Supreme Being and, thus, for worshipping Him alone.'

Muhammad Asad, *The Message of the Quran* (1984), 1

Joseph, Moses and Jesus appear along with the Arabian prophets and sages – unknown to the Bible – Hud, Salih, and Luqman. The theology is an absolute and uncompromising monotheism. As in the Old Testament, the prophets are sent to warn people against straying from the path of righteousness by worshipping false gods. Particularly heinous is the sin of *shirk*, or 'associationism', by which God's majesty is compromised through contamination, as it were, with lesser deities. God's will, majesty, and creative power are continually stressed and celebrated. *Allah* – the Arabic word for God – includes the definite article. It means literally 'the god'. Rather than speculating fruitlessly about his attributes, humans are urged to acknowledge his presence and obey the moral laws and commands deemed to have been revealed to them through successive messengers or prophets. The last of these is Muhammad. God is both transcendent and immanent, the Lord of Creation and One who is nearer to an individual than his 'jugular vein'.

That it is God, rather than Muhammad, who speaks in the Quran is evident from the way many of the utterances are prefixed by the imperative 'Say!', addressed to Muhammad. God refers to himself in the first person singular and plural; but the Prophet is also addressed, apparently, by the Book itself and told about God as a third person. Neal Robinson, a British scholar who has made a detailed analysis of the Quranic style, points out that a sudden shift in pronouns is a characteristic of Arabic rhetoric, arguing that 'God is the implied speaker' throughout the Quran, despite the use of different pronouns.

> With the first person plural He expresses power, majesty and generosity. With the first person singular He safeguards his unity, strikes a note of intimacy, or gives vent to his wrath. With the third person singular He conveys to humankind a universal message in a language which they themselves can re-use.

Other scholars suggest that certain passages are best understood as spoken by angels or by the angel Gabriel. This is especially the case in passages occurring near the beginning of the book, but considered to belong to the later Medinese period of Muhammad's ministry – passages containing detailed prescriptions about marriage, inheritance, and punishment that represent the primary source of Islamic law.

What the Quran lacks for the reader familiar with the Bible or Hindu epics is a coherent narrative structure. Robinson argues that the closest biblical parallels are to the epistles of St Paul, rather than the narratives of Jesus's life as told in the gospels, and he cites the opinion of 18th-century Indian theologian Shah Wali-Allah of Delhi, that the Quran should not be thought of as a book which treats its subject systematically, but rather as a collection of epistles by a king, written for his subjects according to the requirements of the situation. Although there are some individual narratives – notably stories of the prophets, including the so-called 'punishment stories' detailing the direful fates meted out to those who reject God's messengers – the historical discourses are linked thematically rather than chronologically. The biblical narratives addressed to Christians and Jews are presented as reminders and reaffirmations of previous revelations, not as new revelations. Important differences of doctrine, however, emerge in these narratives. The most significant difference from Christian theology is the treatment of the Fall. Satan is punished for his refusal to bow down before Adam; and though Adam sins, as in the biblical story, by eating the forbidden fruit, he repents and is soon restored to favour as God's deputy or vice-regent (*khalifa*), the first prophet in the line of prophets that culminates in Muhammad. There is no doctrine of original sin here, no idea of vicarious atonement. Where there is no original sin, there is no redeemer: the Quranic Jesus is a prophet, born of a Virgin, but he is not the deity incarnate. Where there is neither incarnation nor redeemer, there can be no church, no 'bride' nor 'mystical body' of God. No Eternal Corporation is necessary to guarantee salvation. All that is required of humans is that they obey God's commands and use their intelligence in discerning truth from falsehood, using the Quran as their criterion (*furqan*). God reveals himself, not in a Person, but in what becomes a Text, the words of which are regarded by most Muslims as divine in themselves.

## God's mouthpiece

'Muhammad is the mouthpiece of the divine will, which is communicated to him by Gabriel, and thus, like a confidential official, he stands on the border-line between the king's court and the subjects. Subject he is always. Sometimes he receives messages to convey to the people, or receives commands or exhortations intended for them; sometimes he is directly addressed as the representative of the people, or he receives commands and exhortations intended for them; at other times special exhortations and directions for his own conduct are addressed to him; and at times he steps, as it were, across the line, and facing round upon the people conveys the divine commands and exhortations directly to them.'

W. M. Watt, *Bell's Introduction to the Quran* (Edinburgh, 1970), 67

The verses into which the Quranic *suras* are divided are known in Arabic as *ayas* – the word means 'sign' and is frequently employed in the Quran to demonstrate the existence of God. These 'signs', as well as referring to divine locutions, point to the evidences of God in nature. The theology of the Quran is thus suffused with what became known in Christian theology as the 'argument from design'. The act of reading is in itself an act of devotion.

Although Muhammad is mentioned by name on at least four occasions, there is almost nothing in the Quran, beyond the occasional hint, from which a biography of Muhammad or an account of his ministry can be inferred. In New Testament terms,

3. A page from the Quran: an example of Naskhi script. The text is
Surat al-Nas (114): 'Say: "I seek refuge with the Lord of mankind, King
of mankind, God of mankind, from the evil of the One who whispers
and recoils, Who whispers in the hearts of mankind, of *Jinn* and
mankind."'

it is as if the Epistles were preserved, without any of the four
Gospels or Acts of the Apostles. The Quran 'is as little concerned
with the events of the life of Muhammad as Paul was with the
narrative life of Jesus'.

## Signs and verses

'Each ayah of the Quran is also a sign – in the symbolic or semiotic sense – that points to another level of reality that in turn reaffirms the message of revelation. The believer who seeks to develop a sense of the sacred must thus learn two distinct levels of "language" (*langue*) at the same time – the Arabic text of the Quran itself and the "language" of nature, which is also a manifestation of the speech of God. God created the world as a book; his revelations descended to Earth and were compiled into a book; therefore the human being must learn to "read" the world as a book.'

Vincent J. Cornell, in John L. Esposito (ed.), *Oxford Encyclopedia of the Modern Islamic World* (New York, 1995), iii. 388

The style of the Quran is allusive and elliptical. It is addressed to people already familiar with much of the material it contains. Far from being self-explanatory, it can only be understood by reference to material *outside* itself. The very difficulties it presents as an historical source are a strong *prima facie* case for its authenticity. A work that had been subjected to any kind of redaction would surely show more signs of narrative coherence. One has the impression that Muhammad's words (those articulated in the prophetic mode, when he is supposed to have been possessed by the angel, or God) were regarded from the start as holy artifacts, distinct from his other utterances and worthy to be recorded and stored like sacred relics. Unlike the books of the Old and New Testaments, the Quran suggests itself as unedited 'raw material'. The narrative context in which it occurred – the career of Muhammad – was something that had to be reconstructed in order to approach its multiple meanings. Here, even to the sceptic, chronology conforms to theology. Just as 'God's speech' as delivered by the angel enjoys a higher ontological status than the speeches of the Prophet recorded in the *hadith* literature, so the Prophet's Life appears *after* the testimony of the

Book. Far from Muhammad being the 'author' of the Quran, the Quran is, in a literary-historical sense, the 'author' of Muhammad.

## *Sira* (biography)

Muhammad the Prophet has achieved such eminence as a world-historical figure that it is difficult to conceive of him as having lived out his life in a cultural milieu without historical records, where history is wrapped in myth and historical facts are virtually out of reach. The events of his life, carefully reconstructed from hints and allusions in the Quran and from the oral testimonies of his companions and their successors, were written down more than a century after his death in dramatically different circumstances from those in which his life appears to have been lived. By then, the victorious Arab tribes, under the banner of Islam, had broken out of the Arabian peninsula and conquered much of the civilized world, including Egypt, Palestine, Syria, Mesopotamia, and the highlands of Persia. Much more sophisticated cultures, Zoroastrian, Christian, and Jewish, had come under Arab dominion. Factional feuding had broken out between the tribes while the new cult of Allah and his Arabian prophet faced criticism from the trained theological minds of the older religions.

The earliest Lives of the Prophet that have come down to us are both exegetical and apologetic in purpose. They serve to explain the 'occasions of revelation' – the particular circumstances in the Prophet's life when a verse or passage of the Quran 'came down'. Their treatment of events may be influenced by hindsight or by a retrospective colouring designed to bolster the claims of one of the factions competing for power. They contain a good deal of material of a rhetorical, formulaic, or supernatural character designed to bolster the Chosen One's claims to prophethood in the face of sceptical or prejudiced critics. The lapse of time before the first written sources is considerable. The first biography we have is by Ibn Ishaq who died in 767 CE, 135 years after the death of Muhammad. The version which has come down to us was extracted from a much longer work – probably a 'world history' – by Ibn Hisham (d. 833); other early biographers include al-Waqidi (d. 823) and Ibn Sa'd (d. 845). The annalist Tabari (d. 923) relates material – including the famous 'Satanic Verses' episode – not found in other sources.

The century or more of oral transmission between the life and death of Muhammad and the first biographies makes factual certainty impossible. This has not prevented some scholars, most of them working in Western universities, from formulating highly speculative theories about the origins of Islam. One of the most contentious, originally advanced by the Protestant theologian Günter Lüling, and elaborated more recently by the pseudonymous scholar Christoph Luxenburg, suggests that the Quran may have originated in the strophic hymns of Aramaic-speaking Christianized tribes. These may have been adapted by Muhammad, or retrospectively projected onto him after the Arab conquests. Volker Popp, a numismatist working in Germany, argues – with Luxenburg – that the name 'Muhammad', which appears on the earliest coins and is inscribed on the interior of the Dome of the Rock in Jerusalem (alongside some of the earliest written examples of Quranic texts, dating from the 690s), may actually refer to Jesus: the word 'muhammad' can be read as a passive participle meaning the 'praised' or 'chosen one', raising the possibility that the original Arab conquerors of Palestine were Arian Christians opposed to Byzantine rule. In taking this approach, however, they seem to disregard evidence from non-Muslim sources in which the figures of Muhammad and Jesus are clearly distinct.

What can be said with much more confidence is that the authority of the Quran and of Muhammad became of paramount importance in the disputes and debates that followed the Arab conquest of the Fertile Crescent. The material that found its way into the biographies appears to have been collected according to the same methodology that governed the *hadith*, or 'traditions', the second tier, after the Quran, of the Muslim canon. The men who collected this material may have been as scrupulous in winnowing out reliable from unreliable traditions as circumstances allowed (see below). Modern critical scholarship, however, is bound to question this methodology. Generally, Muslim scholars are less critical, though not universally so.

The following account provides the barest essentials of a biography that would be elaborated over time to encompass the vast range of the exemplary anecdotes forming the raw material of Islamic law.

Muhammad was born around 570 CE in Makka, the site of an ancient sanctuary, one of several *hawtas*, or shrines, in the region where the warring tribesmen would suspend hostilities during the months of pilgrimage and perform various rituals. Non-Muslims believe the rituals to have included fertility cults such as rain-making which are found in numerous cultures. Muslim tradition holds that the square temple at the centre of the shrine, the Ka'ba, was built by Abraham (Ibrahim) near the place of sacrifice. In the Bible, Abraham proves his devotion to God by offering to sacrifice Isaac, ancestor of the Hebrews, his son with the previously barren Sarah. In the Islamic version, the would-be victim is Ishmael or Isma'il, Abraham's son with the bondwoman Hagar, who lived to become ancestor of the Arabs. The sacrifice is commemorated all over the Muslim world at the 'Id al Adha, or Feast of Sacrifice, which comes at the climax of the *Hajj* or Greater Pilgrimage, when hundreds of thousands of pilgrims flock to the sanctuary to perform the reformed or de-paganized rituals instituted by the Prophet during the final year of his life. In the traditional Muslim view, the paganism prevailing in Makka at the time of the Prophet's birth was not some 'primal' religion evolving towards monotheism, but a manifestation of religious decadence. It was a falling off or backsliding from the original 'Islam' or monotheism of Adam, Abraham, Moses, and other prophets and patriarchs.

Muhammad's tribe, the Quraish, had for several generations been guardians of the sanctuary. Makka was situated near, but not directly on, the overland trade routes linking the Mediterranean with southern Arabia and the Indian Ocean. The caravans that stopped there were making a detour because of the city's holiness. Quraishi monopoly of the shrine was institutionalized through a religious association called the Hums, the 'People of the Shrine', who distinguished themselves from the surrounding bedouin by wearing special clothes. They never left the shrine, refusing to participate in those rituals that took place outside the sacred (*haram*) area. These latter rites included the Standing at Arafat and the invocation of the thunder angel at Muzdalifa, later incorporated by Muhammad into the Hajj ceremonies. The pilgrimage brought a measure of prosperity to the Quraish in addition to the regular products they traded in, leather and raisins. Muhammad's grandfather achieved prestige and renown as provider of food and water for the pilgrims and was responsible for re-digging the famous well of Zamzam – associated in Islamic tradition with Hagar. Orphaned at about 6, Muhammad was brought up by his grandfather and later by his maternal uncle Abu Talib. As a young man, he entered the service of Khadija, a wealthy widow, and made several trading journeys to Syria on her behalf. She was so impressed by him that she married him. Muhammad, who is said to have married at least nine other women, remained faithful to Khadija during her lifetime. Despite her comparatively advanced age of 40, she is supposed to have borne him seven children (including three sons who died in infancy).

### Revelation described

*'By the Star when it plunged!*
*Your companion has not veered from the truth, nor is he misguided.*
*Nor is he giving voice to his fancies.*
*It is but an inspiration, inspired,*
*Taught him by one immense in power, daunting.*

> *He took his stand, being on the upper horizon,*
> *Then drew near and hung suspended,*
> *And was two bows' length, or nearer.*
> *And He revealed to His servant what He revealed.*
> *The mind did not question what it saw,*
> *Do you dispute with him what he saw?*
> *And he saw him a second time,*
> *By the lote-tree of the Extremity,*
> *Near which is the Garden of Refuge,*
> *When there covered the lote-tree that which covered it.*
> *The eye neither veered nor overreached.*
> *He saw some of his Lord's greatest wonders.'*
> Quran 53: 1–18

At the age of about 40, Muhammad began undertaking regular retreats to a cave near Mt Hira outside Makka. Scholars are divided as to whether the religious practices he adopted, including an annual retreat, or *tahannuth*, during the month of Ramadan, were part of the existing pagan culture, or whether he may have adopted the pious practices of Christian anchorites he met on his travels in Syria. By general consent, however, it was after a period of meditation that he received his first revelation. The awesome nature of the experience is captured in the fifty-third *sura* of the Quran (1–18).

Tradition, basing itself on *suras* revealed during the Medinese period, would identify the 'one terrible in power' as the angel Gabriel. Two Western scholars, however, Richard Bell and W. Montgomery Watt, argue that in these verses Muhammad believed himself to have been in the presence of God himself, like Moses on Mt Sinai. A third visionary experience, also alluded to in one of the Quran's Makkan *suras*, is said to have occurred after Khadija's death, when Muhammad was transported by night 'from the sacred Mosque to the furthest Mosque' (17: 1). The reference was elaborated by Muslim tradition into the famous Night Journey, when Muhammad was miraculously transported to Jerusalem on the mythical beast Buraq and thence to heaven where he was instructed by God to institute the five daily prayers governing the Muslim faith. The story is consistent with shamanic experiences in many other cultures and may have been purely visionary.

Khadija accepted Muhammad's message as did his uncle's son 'Ali. For three years, according to Ibn Ishaq, Muhammad refrained from proclaiming the message in public. In a small community such as Makka, the message could not be confined to the family circle.

> People began to accept Islam, both men and women, in large numbers until the fame of it spread throughout Makka, and it began to be talked about. Then God commanded His Apostle to declare the truth of what he had received and to make known His commands to men and call them to Him.

According to Ibn Ishaq, the message of Islam did not create opposition until Muhammad spoke disparagingly of the pagan deities. Western scholars suggest that during the earliest period, Muhammad himself practised some of the rituals of paganism – an interpretation contested by Muslims who insist that Muhammad would never have compromised with paganism. (The issue depends in part on the dating and interpretation of certain Quranic passages such as *sura* 108.)

The same issue arises in the case of the so-called Satanic Verses. According to the annalist Tabari (d. 923 CE), one of the recitations revealed at Makka contained positive references to the Makkan goddesses al-Lat, al-Uzza, and Manat as the three 'high-flying cranes' whose intercession was to be hoped for. The Quraishi opposition was overjoyed, and everyone, Muslim and pagan, joined together in prayer at the shrine. There followed an editorial amendment: a new verse was substituted. The three goddesses 'are but names that you and your forefathers coined: regarding them God sent down no authority' (53: 19–23).

The highly controversial story (which may have been invented, and does not appear in the major *hadith* collections) suggests to the student of religion, if not to every believer, that an evolution may have occurred in Muhammad's perception of God – from the High God of the Arabian pantheon to the Unique God without partners, associates or 'daughters'.

The Quran only hints at the Quraishi opposition to Muhammad; the historians and annalists, writing up to three centuries afterwards, suggest that, in addition to his attacks on idolatry, commercial interests played their part. The opposition is said to have been led by the implacable Abu Lahab, 'father of flames'. Muhammad and his immediate family were protected by Abu Talib. But some of his poorer followers were treated extremely badly, notably Bilal, the Abyssinian slave whose powerful and sonorous voice would make him the first *muezzin*. Fearful for their safety and fidelity to the cause, Muhammad sent some of the early converts to Abyssinia, whose Christian ruler provided protection and resisted an attempt by the Quraish to have them returned to Makka. Muhammad, his clan, and those of his followers who remained in Makka were subjected to a boycott with a view to excluding them from the city's commercial life. The boycott encountered resistance from among the pagan

## Depicting the Prophet

In the first edition of this book, this space contained an illustration from the famous manuscript of Rashid al-Din's *Universal History* (1307) in Edinburgh University Library. The picture shows the Prophet seated in a stylized rocky landscape. The Angel Gabriel, a winged figure wearing an ornate Seljuk crown, approaches him from the left with outstretched arm and pointed forefinger. In the words of the art historian David Talbot Rice, 'The spirit of introverted meditation is convincingly depicted.' Although the illuminated manuscript from Tabriz is widely regarded as a masterpiece and is often reproduced, a small number of readers found the picture blasphemous. In the words of one of them: 'There is definitely no human being that can ever depict the beauty and grandeur of his [the Prophet's] countenance.' There is no explicit ban on figurative art in the Quran, but popular Muslim tradition became strongly iconophobic and manuscripts containing Muhammad's image have often been defaced.

Quraish; but just as it looked like collapsing Muhammad's uncle Abu Talib died.

Muhammad's wife Khadija died the same year. Two of his main human supporters were removed. With Khadija, his devoted wife and confidante, he shared his troubles. Abu Talib protected him from the hostility of his tribe. Deprived of his support, Muhammad was increasingly exposed to the ridicule and hostility of Abu Lahab and the Quraishi aristocracy. His followers, apart from a few prestigious converts like Abu Bakr, 'Umar ibn al-Khattab, and 'Uthman ibn 'Affan – the latter a member of the important Umayyad clan – were mostly from among the poorer and less influential elements in a society where wealth, prestige, and lineage were bound up together. Nevertheless, Muhammad's own prestige and reputation as a preacher extended to neighbouring districts. Bedouins who heard him at the local fairs and markets were impressed – especially a group of visitors from Yathrib, an oasis settlement about 275 miles north-east of Makka. The settlement had been divided along tribal lines, with bitter feuding between the clans, three of which, the Banu Quraiza, the Banu Qainuqa and the Banu Nadir, had adopted a form of Judaism (just as some Arab tribes living in and around the Syrian desert adopted versions of Christianity). A delegation invited Muhammad to Yathrib (later renamed al Madina, the City of the Prophet) to act as mediator. In the year 622 CE, about twelve years after the beginning of the Prophet's mission, the Muslims made their migration (*hijra*) to Madina. The Muslim calendar is dated from the year of the Hijra (or Hegira, as it is sometimes spelled in older English texts).

The Madinese *suras* of the Quran provide rather more historical data about the Arabian Prophet's career than those dated from the Makkan period. There are references to his raids on the Quraishi caravans when God permits fighting in the sacred month of Rajab (2: 217); and to the major victory of Badr (624 CE) when God is described as helping the Muslims with a host of angels. (The Battle of Uhud the following year, when the Muslims suffer a setback, is also alluded to (3: 122–3)). There are allusions to Muhammad's relations with the other communities of Madina: the Ansar, or Helpers, who aided the Muslim emigrants, the Munafiqun or Hypocrites who are opportunistic in their support for the Muslims and berated for their disloyalty; and the Jews or Sons of Israel who are derided for their errors and evidently punished for their treachery (33: 26).

These and numerous other allusions to events which apparently occurred are fleshed out by *hadith* reports transmitted over more than a century and included in the *sira*. The Prophet acts as peacemaker in Madina between rival tribal factions, the Aws and Khazraj and their Jewish allies. The Jewish tribes may have been established longer in the oasis and owned most of the date palms. 'The prosperous farms belonged to the Jews', says a 10th-century text, the *Kitab al-Aghani*. But the bedouin Arabs, as is often the case, have the military power. The Jewish tribes find themselves allied to rival Arab factions. As peacemaker, the Prophet enacts a document known as the '*umma* document', or Charter of Madina, regulating the political relationship between the Emigrants, the Helpers, and the Jews. All disputes must be referred to 'God and Muhammad'; the Madinese will form a single community (*umma*) that includes a number of Jewish tribes, who are nonetheless entitled to their own religion (*din*) provided they do not act treacherously.

Muhammad's relations with the Jews of Madina are as crucial for the interpretation of early Islam as his relations with the pagan Quraish. He respects their monotheism and accepts a common patriarchal-spiritual lineage from Abraham, a true *hanif,* or monotheist. The Muslim chroniclers state, however, that, while temporarily accepting Muhammad's political leadership, the Jews of Madina reject him as a prophet in their tradition and that after the victory of Badr, when Muhammad's position is greatly strengthened, his relations with them start to deteriorate. A marketplace dispute leads to the expulsion of the Banu Qainuqa; two years later, they are followed by the Banu Nadir, accused of plotting to murder the Prophet. The following year, the men of the Banu Quraiza are massacred, and their women taken into slavery, after intriguing with the Makkans during the 'Battle of the Ditch', a siege lasting several weeks when the Quraishi cavalry are kept at bay by a series of trenches ordered by the Prophet on the advice of his Persian follower Salman al-Farisi. None of these Jewish clans, whose names appear in the Prophet's biographies, are mentioned in the '*umma* document', considered by some scholars to be of an earlier date, suggesting that stories of his conflicts with the Jews were the outcome of religious polemics occurring at a later time.

In the traditional narrative, the political deterioration in relations with the Jews is complemented by developments on the religious front. The Quranic 'recitation', it has been suggested, becomes 'scripturalized', treated as a book comparable to the Jewish Torah or Christian *Injil* (Gospel). The latter is conceived as a 'holy book' as distinct from an account – or series of accounts – of a holy life. The *qibla* – direction of prayer – changes from Jerusalem to Makka. The Makkan sanctuary and part of the Makkan pagan tradition, are reappropriated in stages and given new meanings within the monotheistic, Abrahamic paradigm. In the sixth year of the Hijra, Muhammad attempts the lesser pilgrimage, or *'Umra*, leading a party of Emigrants and Helpers and some of the bedouin tribesmen. The Makkans stop them from entering the sacred area; but a truce is negotiated under which the Madinans will be able to perform the pilgrimage the following year. Muhammad benefits from the peace on his southern flank to turn his attention to the rebellious Jewish tribes at the oases of Khaibar and Fadak, suspected of being in league with the Makkans. Under the terms of surrender, the Jews continue to work their plantations, giving half their produce to the Muslims. After his return, the Makkans honour the agreement, and Muhammad is able to lead a band of Muslims to perform the *'Umra*. However, the following year (628 CE) the truce breaks down, and in January 630 he returns to the sacred city in strength. Taken by surprise, the Makkans offer no resistance. Their leader, Abu Sufyan, has been captured by the Muslims, and decides to save himself by submission to Islam.

### Idolaters attacked

*Once the sacred months are shorn, kill the polytheists wherever you find them, arrest them, imprison them, besiege them, and lie in wait for them at every site of ambush. If they repent, perform the prayer and pay the alms, let them go on their way: God is All-Forgiving, Compassionate to each. If a polytheist seeks your protection, grant him protection until he hears the speech of God, then escort him to where he feels safe. For they are a people of no understanding.'*

(Quran 9: 5–6)

After circumambulating the Ka'ba and touching the Black Stone with his stick, Muhammad enters the temple and smashes the 360 idols therein, sparing only two icons of Jesus and Mary. (One chronicler, al-Azraqi, states he destroyed them miraculously, merely pointing his stick at them.) Other idols in the vicinity are destroyed, including that of the female deities al-Uzza, Manat, and al-Lat. The Prophet remains in the area of Makka and defeats a hostile bedouin confederation before making a second '*Umra* to the shrine. An expedition launched to the north engages a Byzantine army at Tabuk near present-day Aqaba. The Muslim *umma* is now the greatest force in the Arabian peninsula. During the year 630 CE – the Year of Delegations – most of the tribes submit; the remaining pagans are allowed the four trucial months in which to make up their minds. After that, they may be killed with impunity.

The Muslim *umma* has in effect become a religious state or polity. Previously, Muhammad had signed treaties with non-believers and even shared the booty of his campaigns with them. Now submission to Islam becomes the criterion of membership. In the last year of his life, 632 CE, Muhammad makes what becomes known as the Pilgrimage of Farewell. Pagans are excluded, and the rites of *Hajj* and *Umra*, originally two separate pagan festivals falling in spring and autumn, are compounded. The intercalary month by which the Arabs adjusted the lunar months to the solar year is abolished, severing the connection between the religious rituals and the seasons. Henceforth, the pilgrimage and the Feast of Sacrifice, the central events of the Islamic calendar, will regress through the seasons, forming a complete cycle approximately every 33 years. Muhammad returns to Madina. Here he falls ill, and unexpectedly dies in the arms of the 18-year-old 'Aisha. God's revelations cease.

## Hadith 'traditions'

Often translated as 'traditions', the *hadiths* are really discrete anecdotes about the Prophet's sayings and actions, originally passed down orally and later compiled into written texts. The Prophet's biography – as already stated – was constructed using the same methodology as the *hadiths*, with the biographers scrupulously retaining different versions of the same events and citing their sources. At first glance, the method has a transparency that is lacking in the formation of other scriptures, including the Gospels. Rather than wielding their editorial scalpels, crafting a single consistent narrative out of the oral materials available to them, the *hadith* collectors appear to have sifted every anecdote, report, and story according to very different criteria. What mattered was not so much the plausibility or coherence of the story but the reliability of the sources.

## Tolerance exemplified

'Two persons, a Muslim and a Jew, quarrelled. The Muslim said, "By Him Who gave Muhammad superiority over all the people!" The Jew said, "By Him Who gave Moses superiority over all the people!" At that the Muslim raised his hand and slapped the Jew on the face. The Jew went to the Prophet and informed him of what had happened between him and the Muslim. The Prophet sent for the Muslim and asked him about it. The Muslim informed him of the event. The Prophet said, "Do not give me superiority over Moses, for on the Day of Resurrection all the people will fall unconscious and I will be one of them, but I will be the first to gain consciousness, and will see Moses standing and holding the side of the Throne [of Allah]. I will not know whether [Moses] has also fallen unconscious and got up before me, or Allah has exempted him from that stroke."'

Bukhari, bk. 41 3: 593

The *hadith* collectors were aware from the first that spurious stories about the Prophet were circulating – often to support rival positions in the disputes and struggles for power that followed Muhammad's death. There is a *hadith*, which may or may not be authentic, according to which the Prophet is related to have said: 'He who deliberately tells lies about me will have to seek for himself a place in Hell.' Aware of the pitfalls, the *hadith* transmitters went to great lengths to establish the reliability of the transmitters, thoroughly investigating their characters. They developed a 'science of men' in which only the most honourable and trustworthy individuals came to be considered appropriate vehicles for the sacred task of reporting the Prophet's sayings and deeds. *Hadiths* were graded into varying degrees of reliability: 'sound' (*sahih*), 'good' (*hasan*), or 'weak' (*da'if*). Six collections came to acquire canonical status, with two of these – the *sahihain* or 'two sound ones' of al-Bukhari (d. 870) and Muslim ibn al-Hajjaj (d. 875) – considered as second in importance only to the Quran.

Despite the efforts of the scholars, the volume of *hadiths* continued to swell and modern critics, both Muslim and non-Muslim, have come to doubt whether the methodology was really reliable, given the long period of oral transmission before *hadiths* came to be written down. In India the modernist scholar Sayyid Ahmad Khan (d. 1898) began to question the authenticity of *hadith* in the 19th century; his associate Chirag 'Ali (d. 1898) took the view that the 'vast flood of traditions soon formed a chaotic sea. Truth and error, fact and fable, mingled together in an indistinguishable confusion.' In the West, scholars such as Ignaz Goldziher and Joseph Schacht argued that the *isnads* – the chains of transmitters – had a tendency to 'grow backwards': that is to say anecdotes or reports originating at a later date with a Companion or Successor *after* the Arab conquest of the Fertile Crescent were given *isnads* tracing them back to the Prophet in order to endow them with an authority they would otherwise have lacked. In the same vein, the sections containing the content of some *hadiths* (known as the *matn*) were identified as anachronistic: Schacht in particular argued that many fail to appear in the course of legal discussions at a time when reference to them would have been imperative.

Nowadays, conservative Muslims have tended to ignore these criticisms, or to regard them as typically 'Western' attacks on Islam fuelled by religious or cultural animosity. Earlier generations were a good deal more sceptical about the character and quality of the transmitters than their descendants came to be.

## Birth control

'We took some women captives, and when we had sex with them we practised withdrawal (*coitus interruptus:* Arab. '*azl*) so as not to have children with them. We asked the Messenger of God about this and he said "Is that what you did?" Then he repeated three times: "There is not a soul who is to be born for the day of resurrection, but that he will be born."'

Al-Bukhari, ed. Krehl and Juynboll, *kitab al-jam'i al-sahih* (Leiden 1868–1908), vol. iii. 448, cited in John Alden Williams (ed.), *Islam* (London, 1961), 86. (I have slightly modernized this translation.)

## Authenticity of *hadith*

The scepticism of early commentators regarding the authenticity of the *hadith* literature is illustrated by a revealing story related by the traditionist 'Umar ibn Habib, who became involved in an argument at the court of the famous Caliph Harun al-Rashid (786–809) over the merits of one of the most celebrated *hadith* transmitters, the Companion Abu Huraira, regarded as an unimpeachable source of the Prophet's *sunna* (custom). When his antagonists began to cast doubt on Abu Huraira's reliability 'Umar could contain himself no longer – despite the fact that the all powerful Caliph supported their position. After announcing that the *hadith* in question was genuine, and that Abu Huraira was a trustworthy transmitter, 'Umar received an angry look from the Caliph. When summoned to the royal presence, the Caliph said to him: 'O 'Umar ibn Habib, nobody has ever confronted me with arguments refuting and rejecting my opinion as you have!' 'O Prince of the Believers', the terrified 'Umar responded, 'Verily in what you say, and in the argument you used, there lay disrespect for the Messenger of God and for what he has brought us. If his Companions are thought of as liars, the whole *shari'a* becomes null and void; the inheritance prescriptions, as well as

> the rulings concerning fasting, the prayer ritual, divorce and
> marriage, all these ordinances will then be abolished and will no
> longer be accepted.' The Caliph lapsed into silence. Then he said:
> 'You have given me new insights. May God grant you a long life,
> 'Umar ibn Habib.' And he ordered that the scholar be given
> 10,000 dirhams.
>
> Adapted from G. H. A. Juynboll, *Muslim Tradition*
> (Cambridge University Press, 1983), 197–8

## The elaboration of Muhammad's image

Authentic or otherwise, the *hadiths* became the vehicle by
which the Prophet's example became the model of human
behaviour for countless numbers of Muslims over the centuries.
*Imitatio Christi* meant imitating Christ's suffering and
adopting, ideally, his gospel of love. There are no detailed
prescriptions in the New Testament about how Jesus dressed,
ate, walked, cleaned his teeth, or generally comported himself,
although it may be true that a composite image of his
*appearance* eventually transmits itself through Christian
iconography, as does that of the Buddha and numerous Hindu
deities. *Imitatio Muhammadi* meant following the Prophet's
example in every aspect of life, from ethical conduct to diet. In
Islam, two- or three-dimensional representations of created
beings were generally forbidden (lest the artist be seen to
appropriate God's creative power) and even those traditions that
allowed representation in later times usually depicted the
Prophet as faceless or veiled, so holy was his presence. Yet his
model – idealized, no doubt, and infused with the values and
aspirations of later generations – was disseminated, both orally
and through the *hadith* literature, to become a cultural and
religious icon as powerful as Christ or the Buddha, the image of
*al-insan al-kamil*, the perfect or complete human being in both
his worldly and spiritual aspects.

## Muhammad's appearance

'Muhammad was middle-sized, did not have lank or crisp hair, was not fat, had a white, circular face, wide black eyes and long eyelashes. When he walked, he walked as though he went down a declivity. He had the 'seal of prophecy' [a dark mole or fleshy protruberance the size of a pigeon's egg] between his shoulder blades... He was bulky. His face shone like the moon in the night of full moon. He was taller than middling stature, yet shorter than conspicuous tallness. He had thick curly hair. The plaits of his hair were parted... Muhammad had a wide forehead and fine, long, arched eyebrows which did not meet. Between his eyebrows there was a vein which distended when he was angry. The upper part of his nose was hooked; he was thick bearded, had smooth cheeks, a strong mouth and his teeth were set apart. He had thin hair on his chest. His neck was like the neck of an ivory statue, with the purity of silver. Muhammad was proportionate, stout, firm-gripped, even of belly and chest, broad-chested, and broad-shouldered.'

Annemarie Schimmel, *And Muhammad Is His Messenger* (Chapel Hill: University of North Carolina Press, 1985), 34

The image of the Prophet, literary rather than visual, radiates throughout the Muslim world. Perhaps the very restriction on pictorial representation aids cultural diffusion, allowing peoples of different races and ethnicities to internalize its essential features – courage, calm, compassion, *gravitas*, and holiness. Muhammad claimed no superhuman qualities for himself. 'Say... "I am merely a warner, and a herald of good tidings to a people who believe"' (7: 188). Yet the *siras* are full of supernatural episodes which would later acquire elaborate legendary accretions. The story emanating from the opening of *sura* 94, 'Have We not soothed your heart? Have We not relieved you of the burden that weighed upon your back?', is elaborated in *hadiths* about angelic visitors who take him to a mountain top, open his breast, and remove the heart, which is cleansed with snow and replaced after a 'black speck, filled with blood', representing 'Satan's part in him', has been removed. Thus guaranteed, the Prophet's sinlessness makes him the immaculate source of emulation for later generations. However, as Annemarie Schimmel pointed out, there was no official doctrine concerning the Prophet's sinlessness in the earliest days of Islam, and the first generation of historians and commentators were less concerned than their successors would be with exonerating him from taking any part in the pagan rituals of Makka before Allah guided him to the worship of the one true God.

A similar edifice of legend and poetic imagery accrues around the opening of the fifty-fourth *sura*: 'The hour has drawn near, and the moon is split!' While modernists and some other commentators sought to demythologize the phrase by pointing to its eschatological context – along with other marvels as the Day of Judgement approaches, the moon will split – most of the early commentators saw it as a reference to an actual event described in several *hadiths* attributed to the Prophet's Companions, according to which the moon appeared one night as if split into separate parts. In popular tradition as in mystical poetry, the 'splitting of the moon' becomes one of Muhammad's greatest miracles, celebrated in Sindhi, Punjabi, Swahili, and other Muslim languages. In other miracle stories, the Prophet emulates the Quranic Jesus by breathing life into a bird of stone, produces rain after drought or water from between his fingers, and causes a solitary barren sheep to provide enough milk for his thirsty companions and himself. Another food miracle in which 1,000 people are fed from a single sheep recalls the 'Feeding of the Five Thousand' in the New Testament. Camels and wild beasts prostrate themselves before Muhammad, knowing him to be a messenger sent by God, along with inanimate things such as rocks and stones and trees.

The great Persian poet Jami proclaims:

> A little stone, smaller than a rosary's bead
> Recited in his hand with eloquent words the praise of God,
> And those eloquent ones whose hearts were black as stone,
> Were unison in silence.

## Muhammad as model

'Know that the key to happiness is to follow the Sunna and to imitate the Messenger of God in all his coming and going, his movements and rest, in his way of eating, his attitude, his sleep and his talk. I do not mean this in regard to religious observance, for there is no reason to neglect the traditions which were concerned with this aspect. I rather mean all the problems of custom and usage, for only by following them unrestricted succession is possible. God has said: "Say: If you love God, follow me, and God will love you" (sura 3: 29), and He has said: "What the messenger has brought – accept it, and what he has prohibited – refrain from it!" (sura 59: 7). That means, you have to sit while putting on trousers, and to stand when winding a turban, and to begin with the right foot when putting on shoes."'

Ghazali, *Ihya 'ulum al Din* 2: 300–44, tr. Leo Zolondek (Leiden: Brill, 1963), cited by Schimmel, 31

Those to whom the Prophet appears in dreams cannot be deceived, for God will not permit Satan to take his form, and on waking their chambers will be filled with the pleasant scent of musk. To allow for imposture – a false vision of the Prophet – would undermine the unity of Islam by inviting accusations and counter-accusations of fraud. By the same logic, the Muslim mystic is denied direct access to divine revelation, for Muhammad is the 'seal' of the prophets, the final revelator sent by God to humankind. Visions of the Prophet are not just *ipso facto* authentic – they guarantee that the mystics and visionaries to whom they are vouchsafed remain within the Islamic fold. Where a mystic or holy man is claimed to have been the recipient of direct revelation – as in the case of Mirza Ghulam Ahmad, founder of the proselytizing Ahmadiya sect – controversy and accusations of heresy will dog his followers.

Muhammad's role as a source of emulation, however, is far from being confined to mystics and visionaries. The physical details of his life – the cut of his beard, the clothes he wore, the food he liked, as reported in the *hadith* literature – came to be seen as models of human comportment and human behaviour. Some people avoided certain foods such as garlic, mangoes, and melons, because he was reported to have disliked them, or because there was no record that he had eaten them. Honey and mutton were cherished because he cherished them; dogs were considered unclean because – according to a well-known *hadith* – 'the angels do not enter a house in which there is a dog or statues'; but cats were approved of because – as he is related to have said – they are among the animals that grace human dwellings. The medieval mind saw in his every activity the perfection of conduct, his every opinion a direct guidance from God.

## Muhammad's inaccessibility

'Our culture can no longer move in this universe it calls magical, superstitious, unreal, irrational, imaginary, marvellous, fabulous and legendary. All this vocabulary conveys difference, rejection, distance and disqualification rather than integration into a comprehensive realm of intelligibility capable of accommodating all the facts and phenomena presented for analysis. The religious experience and historical activity of Muhammad emerges and unfurls precisely in this semiological universe we no longer understand.'

Mohamed Arkoun, *Rethinking Islam: Common Questions, Uncommon Answers*, tr. and ed. Robert D. Lee (Boulder, CO: Westview Press, 1994), 43

Muhammad, like Jesus and the founders of other world religions, is a bridge between myth and history, the realms, respectively, of divine and human action. He inhabits a world where historical activity is surrounded by supernatural forces, where the numinous constantly interpenetrates the dull sublunary world of common sense. To grasp this world in its fullness must lie beyond our capacities as moderns. Scholars of varying disciplines can only hope to analyse fragments of the vast cultural imaginative and historical residue left from the two decades when God addressed humanity – as Muslims see it – through the words of the last of his prophets.

# Chapter 3
# **Divine unicity**

## *Tawhid*: introduction

If there is a single word that can be taken to represent the
primary impulse of Islam, be it theological, political, or
sociological, it is *tawhid* – making one, unicity. Although the
word does not occur in the Quran, the concept it articulates is
implicit in the credal formula *there is no god but God*, and there
are references to the God who is without partners or associates
throughout the holy text. The absolute insistence that it is unicity
above all that defines divinity appears in striking, if ironic,
contrast with the disunity observable in the Muslim world. It is as
if the aspiration to realize divine unicity in terms of the social and
political order is forever destined to wreck itself on the shores of
human perversity.

---

### **God's unity**

*'Say: He is God, Unique,*
*God, Lord Supreme!*
*Neither begetting, nor begotten,*
*And none can be His peer .'*
(Quran *sura* 112)

---

**4. The Dome of the Rock and al-Aqsa Mosque in Jerusalem.**
**A masterpiece in the Byzantine style, the Dome of the Rock proclaimed**
**the unity of God while celebrating the triumph of Islam over**
**Christianity**

The overwhelming stress on God's uniqueness reflects the
polemical context in which early Islam was forged. *Tawhid*
simultaneously challenges Arabian paganism, Zoroastrian
dualism, and the Christian doctrine of divine incarnation in
language that recalls, and deliberately harks back to, the
uncompromising monotheism of the Hebrew prophets. The first
great building constructed by the conquering Arabs in Palestine –
the Dome of the Rock on Jerusalem's Holy Mount – occupies the
site of the Jewish Temple on ground where Jewish tradition
supposes that Abraham sacrificed his son, and where in later
times the Ark of the Covenant came to rest. The exquisite
octagonal building, with its marble cladding and golden dome, is
decorated with Quranic inscriptions proclaiming God's unity and
Muhammad's prophethood. The same inscriptions appear on
the coinage minted by its builder, the Caliph 'Abd al-Malik
(r. 685–705). The new shrine is close to the spot from where
Muhammad is supposed to have ascended to heaven on his Night

Journey, when, according to Islamic tradition, he was received by Abraham and Moses, and taught the duties of prayer. The shrine replaces and supersedes the Temple of Solomon, a portion of which is preserved as the 'Wailing' or Western Wall where Jews worship, and mounts a direct challenge to Christianity, the imperial faith of Byzantium.

## The first sectarian divisions

Unity of empire was seen as the reflection of divine unity, a unity compromised by the errors of the Jews and the false doctrines (divine incarnation, vicarious atonement for sin) of the Christians. Yet from the very first, according to Islam's sacred narrative, that terrestrial unity was compromised by the Muslims themselves. Muhammad's death in 632 CE created a crisis of

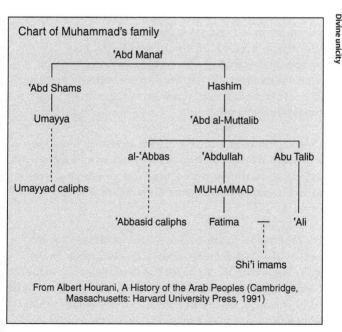

Chart of Muhammad's family

From Albert Hourani, A History of the Arab Peoples (Cambridge, Massachusetts: Harvard University Press, 1991)

authority that has never been resolved. Abu Bakr, his close companion and father of his favourite wife 'Aisha, was proclaimed leader in Medina, following Arab tribal custom. The claims of 'Ali, Muhammad's cousin and son-in-law, his closest male relative, were bypassed on this and two subsequent occasions. Only after the death of 'Uthman did 'Ali come into what his Partisans (Arab. Shi'a) regarded as his lawful inheritance. But by now, it was too late. 'Ali's leadership was contested, and he failed to impose his authority over the whole community. The garrisons based in Iraq supported him; the troops based in Syria under the command of Mu'awiya resisted, and an attempted compromise, promoted by 'Ali in the interests of unity, collapsed in acrimony. Some of 'Ali's supporters were so disillusioned that they left his camp, becoming known as 'Seceders' (*tharijis* – literally, 'those who go out'), a name that became attached to the first separate sect in Islam. One of them, Ibn Muljam, assassinated 'Ali – and so the tragic history of Shi'ism began. 'Ali's eldest son Hasan compromised with Mu'awiya, and retired to live quietly in Medina. It was his younger brother Hussein who, on Mu'awiya's death in 680, raised the standard of revolt, and died on the field of Karbala on the banks of the Euphrates, cut down by the troops of Mu'awiya's son Yazid.

These early disputes were largely, if not exclusively, concerned with power. Who had the right to leadership, by what authority? But they also acquired a distinctively religious colouring as the issue of leadership and authority was perceived as necessary to salvation.

The Imams or leaders in the line of 'Ali demonstrated not the unity of Islam, but rather its opposite. Popular support for the Shi'i cause, among those who felt that the worldly rulers of the Islamic empire had betrayed its message of unity, peace, and social justice, was never lacking. In 749, a Shi'i-inspired movement led to the formation of a new dynasty that moved the capital from

Syria to Iraq. To the disappointment of many of its supporters, however, the new ruler turned out to be a descendant not of 'Ali, but of Muhammad's uncle 'Abbas: closer to the Holy Family than the Umayyads, but not of the Prophet's progeny. This further betrayal inspired the Shi'i Leader of the day, the Imam Ja'far, to adopt a more quietist approach in the manner of Hasan rather than Hussein. Despite their acquiescence in *de facto* reality of non-'Alid power, Shi'i Imams remained a thorn in the side of the new 'Abbasid caliphs. In the sacred history of Shi'ism, each Imam in turn was secretly murdered – usually by poisoning. Eventually, the Twelfth Imam, Muhammad al Muntazar – the Awaited One – disappeared altogether. The Shi'a believed – and still believe – that he will return at the end of time as the messiah (al-Mahdi) to bring peace, justice, and unity to a world torn by corruption, division, and strife. This was a convenient solution to the problem of an underground, but divinely guided, leader: given the doubts that must always surround a succession under such circumstances, was easier to build a consensus around an absent Imam than one who was still living underground.

Thereafter, Shi'ism would oscillate between quietism and activism. Just as the Seceders eventually established separatist communities on the fringes of the Islamic world, in the Tunisian desert, Oman, and Zanzibar, where they are known as Ibadis, so various factions of Shi'a created separate states or polities outside the metropolitan areas: in Tabaristan, Yemen, North Africa, and the Gulf. At times leaders of the Shi'a counselled caution. A doctrine known as *taqiya* – dissimulation – allowed the believers to conceal their true allegiance to the Imams if they feared for their safety: the cruel injustices inflicted on the Family of Muhammad and their followers would have to wait for the return of the Hidden Imam before being rectified. But the eschatological expectations surrounding the Hidden Imam inspired and legitimized revolts, some of which led to permanent changes of government. The example of the Prophet's grandsons Hasan and Hussein, the quietist and the activist, could be invoked to justify either course.

## Other branches of Shi'ism

The followers of the Twelfth Imam, who now number some 80 million in Iran (where Shi'ism is the state religion), Iraq, Afghanistan, Pakistan, Azerbaijan, Syria, Lebanon, Turkey, and the Gulf, are usually known as Imamis or Ithna'asharis ('Twelvers'). A minority sect of the Shi'a, however, claims allegiance to Isma'il, eldest son of the Imam Ja'far whom Twelvers believe to have predeceased his father or to have been passed over. Sometimes known as Seveners, they are generally called Isma'ilis. During the 10th century CE, these Isma'ilis were at the forefront of several revolts inspired by eschatological expectations. In 909, a leader claiming descent from Isma'il proclaimed himself the Mahdi and created a state in North Africa. His son's general successfully invaded Egypt, founding a caliphate there (which became known as the Fatimid caliphate, after the Prophet's daughter). The Fatimids reigned for more than two centuries, until 1171, when they were replaced by the Sunni hero Salah al-Din al-Ayyubi – known to the West as Saladin – liberator of Jerusalem from the Crusaders. Though Egypt was brought back into the Sunni fold, the Isma'ili communities survived in mountain strongholds in Syria, Persia, and Yemen. Their descendants include two prosperous modern groups from India – the Musta'lian Bohras and the Nizari Isma'ilis. The latter are the only group of Shi'a who still claim allegiance to a living Imam – the Imams in the line of the Fatimid Caliph al-Musta'li having also 'disappeared'. The Nizaris, now widely distributed in India, Pakistan, East Africa, Europe, and North America, as well as western China and central Asia, believe that their current Imam, known by his Persian title of Aga Khan, is the forty-ninth Imam in direct line of descent from 'Ali.

Another important branch of the Shi'a allegiance are the Zaidis of Yemen, numbering some three millions, who recognize Zaid ibn 'Ali (grandson of Hussein who died at Karbala), instead of his brother Muhammad al-Baqir as fifth imam. Other surviving off-shoots of the Shi'a include the Druzes of Lebanon, who describe themselves as Unitarians (*muwahhidun*), laying particular stress on *tawhid* as taught by sixth Fatimid Caliph al-Hakim bi Amr Allah (996–1021), the 'Alawis of Syria (also known as Nusairis), who went further than other Shi'a groups by proclaiming 'Ali's divinity. Though a minority in Syria; under the regime of Hafez al-Asad and his son Bashar, they effectively controlled the ruling Ba'th Party and the security forces, until challenged in the turbulent 'Arab Spring' of 2011.

## The passion plays

'Elsewhere, in towns but above all in villages, the *taziya* is held. This religious theatre is so extraordinary, so popular and so spontaneous. It gathers all around a scene improvised in the open air (or in the *husseiniya*). The spectators and actors are interchangeable: everyone knows Yazid, 'Ali, Akbar, Zeinab and Hazrat Abbas... they are the ones in the village who can read and have decked themselves out for the occasion in the costumes of the drama. They have their script in their hands and the director asks them to read their part, handing each the microphone in his turn. There is magic, with horses stampeded through the midst of it all, firecrackers that explode during the battle, the hand of Abbas that flies through the air before managing to get water from the Euphrates (symbolised by a bath-tub) to assuage the thirst of Hussein's companions. There is blood, the clashing of sabres, whirled round over heads, the beating of drums and the sound of death cries.'

Yann Richard, *Shi'ite Islam* (Oxford: Blackwell, 1995), 99

Issues of leadership rather than doctrine were originally at the heart of the dispute between the Shi'a and what become the Sunni majority. But over time, disputes about politics acquire a theological dimension. The 'massacre' of Karbala, a fight between rival clans that only lasts a day and results in a few dozen dead, becomes the defining belief of Shi'ism, an emblem of suffering and martyrdom. Re-enacted on the anniversary in every Shi'i village with processions of bloody flagellants who punish themselves for the betraying of the Prophet's grandson, it does for Shi'ism what Christ's Passion does for Catholicism: it reconciles the believer to the world's injustices, while offering the promise of redemption. The Imams acquire a supernatural dimension. They are the sources of esoteric scriptural knowledge, bearers of the Divine Light of Truth since the creation, who alone can understand and decode the meanings of scripture. In the Twelver and Musta'lian Isma'ili traditions, the absent Imam's authority is exercised on his behalf by religious professionals or deputies. Among the Twelvers, this delegation has led to the elaboration of a clerical hierarchy comparable to the Christian priesthood, without possessing its formal sacerdotal powers.

## The Shi'i Imamate

'The Imamate is to some extent the consequence and the application of the principle of justice to the guidance of humankind. God, who created men, could not let them go to their perdition. That is why He sent them the prophets, the last of whom was Muhammad, to guide them along the path of justice and truth. But after the death of the last prophet it was unthinkable that God in His wisdom should leave men to their own devices without there being, in every era, a spiritual guarantor, proof of the truth of the revelation, to direct the community: this is the Imam, the "Guide". As he plays a fundamental role in the relations between God and men, the Imam cannot be chosen by fallible men and left to the vicissitudes of history: he must fulfil certain conditions of principle, be perfectly learned in religious matters, be absolutely just and equitable, be perfect, free from any fault, be the most perfect man of his time; it is inconceivable that someone more perfect should obey another less perfect... The Imam is designated by a supernatural investiture (*nass*) coming from God by the

> intermediary of the Prophet or the Imam who has preceded him: he receives his authority from on high. Thus the infallible Imam links the human community with the invisible world.'
>
> Richard, *Shi'ite Islam*, 6

## *Tawhid* in early Islamic thought

For the Sunni *'ulama*, the doctrine of God's unicity has ramifications primarily in terms of law. It is not for humans to speculate on the nature of God. Rather, it is their duty to obey his commands. In its most extreme formulation, human laws have no authority underpinning them. Only the laws of God, embodied in the Shari'a, demand obedience. Such insistence on giving priority to God's commands as distinct from his Nature or Being, however, was never enough to satisfy speculative minds or the mystical orientation of those who sought to penetrate the inner experience of the divine. Early theological debates centred on such questions as the status of sinners, free will and predestination, God's justice, and the anthropomorphic attributions of God in the Quran.

The issue of sinners involved the fundamental question 'Who is a Muslim?' The first radical splinter group, the Khawarij, or Seceders, believed that serious sinners such as adulterers had *ipso facto* excluded themselves from the community and could no longer be considered Muslims. At the other end of the spectrum a group known as the Murjia, whose best-known spokesman was Abu Hanifa, founder of the most liberal of the schools of law, argued that anyone making the profession of faith (the Shahada) was a Muslim: their sins would be judged by God. This doctrine encouraged conversions to Islam among peoples on the fringes, such as central Asian nomads; but it made the need for legal enforcement less compelling: if everything is to be left to the judgement of God, what is the point of implementing the law? To this the learned men among the People of the Sunna or 'traditionalists' had their answer. The sinner can still be a Muslim, but there are different degrees of faith and a person's standing in the community (and, by extension, the desirable aim of creating a virtuous society) is determined by good works.

Arguments over sin inevitably lead to the broader question of free will and predestination. Does God know in advance who is going to sin? Is he bound by his own rules of justice? Must he reward virtue and punish wrongdoing? Or does this impinge on his freedom of action, his omnipotence? The argument about God's justice was deeply bound up with the question of God's unicity and with the status of revelation itself. In one of the earliest passages of the Quran revealed to the Prophet in Makka 'God' – speaking through Muhammad – curses Muhammad's chief Quraishi opponent, Abu Lahab, for his persistent opposition, and predicts for him a roasting in hell (Quran 111). If Abu Lahab was a free agent, able to choose between acceptance and rejection of God's message, it followed that the Quran must already have been 'created' when this message was 'sent down'. To suggest otherwise would be to argue that God had already predetermined Abu Lahab's fate, depriving him of freedom of action. The doctrine of the Created Quran, however, ran into powerful opposition from the traditionalists, who saw it as derogating from the idea of the Quran as God's speech. The group of theologians known as the Mu'tazila who espoused the doctrine of the Created Quran adopted a rationalist style of argumentation influenced by the Greek philosophers. For them divine unicity was compromised by the doctrine of an Uncreated Quran. The argument was further complicated by the presence in the Quran of certain anthropomorphic expressions, such as God's face, hands, eyes, throne, and so forth. For the Mu'tazila who were also known as the People of Unity and Justice, literal interpretations of such expressions smacked of *shirk* – 'associationism' or 'idolatry': the association of lesser, i.e. created, beings with God, detracting from his transcendental 'otherness'. Expressions such as God's 'face' must be understood as referring to his essence, his 'eyes' as his capacity to see.

The rationalist tendency held sway at the 'Abbasid court under the Caliph al-Mamun (813–33) who imposed an inquisition-type system, the *mihna*, according to which government officials were obliged to declare their allegiance to the doctrine of the Created Quran. One who refused to do so, despite imprisonment and torture, was Ahmad Ibn Hanbal, the traditionist, who subsequently became a hero for the anti-Mu'tazili People of the Sunna and Community.

In 849, under one of al-Mamun's successors, the policy was reversed. Theological underpinning for a compromise between the rationalists and traditionalists was supplied by a former Mu'tazili, Abu al-Hasan al-Ash'ari (d. 935). Ash'ari and his followers insisted that the Quran was uncreated and that God has foreknowledge of human action, as described in the Quran. He argued, however, that God's omniscience and human responsibility could be accommodated by a doctrine of 'acquisition' whereby God creates the power for people to 'acquire' actions created by him at the instant of action. The Ash'aris were satisfied that their doctrine preserved God's monopoly of creation, hence his unicity. Ash'ari denounced the Mu'tazili attempts to allegorize or de-anthropomorphize the Quranic deity's attributes by stating that they existed in addition to his essence. If the divine will were perceived as one with the divine essence (as the Mu'tazila argued), then divine unicity was indeed compromised, for God's freedom of choice was called into question. Ultimately, for the Ash'aris, God is inaccessible to human reason. God makes himself known only through revelation, and the terms in which he chooses to reveal himself (including his throne, his hands, etc.) must be accepted 'without asking how' – *bila kaif*. This phrase, a key term in Ash'ari theology, 'leaves to God the understanding of his own mystery'.

## The Sunni consensus

For centuries, Ash'ari theology held sway over what would become known as Sunni Islam. With the débâcle of the *mihna* the attempted fusion of religious and political authority in the caliphate was seen to have failed. Religious leadership remained for the most part in the hands of the *'ulama* – a class of religious scholars whose authority was based on their knowledge of scripture, but not on hierocratic or spiritual power. There is no clear 'pecking order' among the Sunni *'ulama*: just as among American Protestants virtually anyone with a basic theological training can become a preacher, so amongst Sunnis 'any qualified [Islamic] lawyer can declare whether something is against Islamic law, so there can be as many versions of "orthopraxy" as there are jurists'. Generally, decentralized religious authority (as in American Protestantism) tends towards conservatism. Without a cult of divinely inspired leadership the text becomes paramount, and even if the text itself is deemed to be divine, interpretation is most likely to proceed in the safety of well-worn grooves.

## Theosophical speculations

The Sunni consensus may have opted for the safety of focusing on God's commands rather than indulging in speculation about his nature; but after their first encounters with Helleno-Christian thought some Muslim intellectuals refused to be put off by *bila kaif*, going to considerable lengths to reconcile the Quranic deity with the God of the philosophers. As they developed an increasingly sophisticated discourse, the Islamic philosophers gradually moved away from the 'Quranic God who creates, acts in time, guides mankind and who can in some way, albeit indirectly, be known' towards 'an utterly remote, unknowable God who does not even create'. The systems they constructed vary as do their terminologies. Common to most of them, however, are ideas of emanation derived from Neoplatonism and in particular the philosopher Plotinus (*c.* 204–70 CE), who defined God, 'the One [who] is in truth beyond all statement and affirmation', in negative as well as positive terms. This *via negativa* is consistent with the Islamic credal formula, which begins with the negative *'There is no god…'*; God's positive dimension could still be approached through his 'great names' of which there are ninety-nine in the Quran. Creation comes not directly from God but through a series of emanations – the First Intellect, the Second Intellect, the First Heaven and so forth – that correspond to the various medieval cosmologies. God himself remains intact, uninfringed upon, unexplained, and inexplicable. The Persian philosopher Ibn Sina (Avicenna) (979–1037), arguing that God has knowledge of generalities but not particulars, emphasized the gulf between the philosophical god and the God of Quranic theology, to the annoyance of the conservatives.

However, speculation about God was allowed to flourish under the patronage of the Isma'ili Imams who elevated reason or intellect to the highest level beneath the unknown and unknowable deity. This God is not in himself the cause of things: his being is beyond the whole chain of existence, of cause and effect. Isma'ili cosmologies varied in their details, but they shared common features, including an emphasis on a Transcendent Deity, unknown and unknowable; a system of emanations corresponding to the Isma'ili hierarchy with the Imam at its head and a cyclical view of history according to which each era has its prophet and his 'silent' companion who knows the inner meanings of the scriptures. Unabashed elitists, the Isma'ilis developed their system against a background of differential hermeneutics whereby the literal or exoteric meanings of the Quran were accessible to the many, while the 'inner' or esoteric meanings were known only to the few. For example Isma'ili writers would interpret the Quranic descriptions of heaven and hell as referring to states of being rather than physical places of bliss or torment. The true meaning of scripture was known to the Imam and the *da'is*, or missionaries, appointed by him. Though not a 'paid-up member' of the Isma'ili movement, Ibn Sina may be said to have been a fellow-traveller. Likewise, the great Spanish philosopher Ibn Rushd (Averroës) (1126–98) has been described as 'almost a closet Isma'ili' in his acceptance of differential hermeneutics. For Ibn Rushd, the ordinary people are required to accept the Quran in its literal or exoteric sense lest they be led into *kufr* (disbelief) whereas the philosophers have much more discretion in interpreting scriptural truth. Ibn Rushd, who in addition to being a philosopher acted as a judge charged with the implementation of the Shari'a, has been accused of 'double standards' in preaching 'one truth for the masses, and another for the elect'. A more tactful way of putting it, however, is to say that, like the Isma'ilis, 'he is a proponent of a multivocal expression of truth'. It is generally accepted that Ibn Rushd's influence was greater in the medieval West than in the Muslim world.

## Sufism

It was not only the philosophers and intellectuals who rejected literalistic interpretations of scripture. The mystically inclined Sufis – named after the coarse shirts of wool (*souf*) worn by some early adepts – rejected or de-emphasized outward or formalistic forms of observance in favour of a style of pietism that sought to apprehend the reality of God's unity through direct experience. Scholars have suggested that early Sufis may have been influenced by mystical tendencies among Eastern Christians, gnostics (who abounded in the ancient Near East in important intellectual centres such as Alexandria), central Asian shamans and even yogis from India. But there are many Quranic passages that lend themselves to a mystical interpretation, most famously a verse in the Sura of Light (24: 35) which dwells on the theme of divine radiance.

### The Sura of Light

*'God is the Light of the heavens and the earth*
*His light is like a niche in which is a lantern,*
*The lantern in a glass,*
*The glass like a shimmering star,*
*Kindled from a blessed tree,*
*An olive, neither of the East nor of the West,*

*Its oil almost aglow, though untouched by fire.*
*Light upon light!*
*God guides to His light whomever He wills,*
*And strikes parables for mankind.*
*God has knowledge of all things.*
(Quran 24: 35)

Among the earliest Sufi adepts was the famous Rabiʿa al-ʿAdawiya, a poet of Basra who defied convention by eschewing marriage, and would run through the streets of the city with a torch in one hand and a jug of water in the other: 'I am going to light fire in Paradise and pour water onto Hell, so that both veils may be taken away from those who journey towards God [that] they may look towards their Sustainer without any object of hope or motive of fear.' The pure, disinterested love of God, without hope of reward or fear of punishment, is the leitmotif of Sufism throughout the centuries. The Sufi adept, through spiritual disciplines such as yogic breathing while pronouncing the pronoun 'He' (*huwa*) in remembrance of God, ultimately aspires to the state of *fana*, union with God. But Sufism also influences less mystically oriented souls, such as the great jurist and theologian Abu Hamid al-Ghazali (d. 1111) and Hasan al-Banna (1906–49) founder of the Muslim Brotherhood. Ghazali left his teaching post in Baghdad and spent several years as a Sufi travelling to Syria and Palestine before writing his famous *Ihya ʿUlum al-Din* – 'The Revitalization of the Religious Sciences' – a book which infuses the strict orthopraxy of Sunnism with a powerful dose of mystical piety, so that every activity from defecation to prayer becomes in its own way a 'remembrance of God'. The *Ihya* was Hasan al-Banna's bedside reading. With Ghazali, as with other writers belonging to the so-called 'sober' Sufis, the law remains the frame through which mystical feeling must manifest itself. But mystical enthusiasm can also take radical antinomian forms which transgress the rules of the Shariʿa and sometimes scandalize the pious.

### God's love

'The Sufis teach that the natural love of humans for each other is necessary to show one the way to the love of God. The lover who "passes away" has no carnal soul left...the friends of God, by loving one another, bear witness to the reality of love, as do animals and the works of the Divine Artist, which manifest Universal Beauty. The lovers of God reach either unitive fusion with him (*ittihad*, a concept condemned in later Sufism) or the "station" of experiencing God's Uniqueness (*tawhid*) which means reaching him, so that he seems both to be and not to be in and through everything.'

Julian Baldick, *Mystical Islam: An Introduction to Sufism* (London: I.B. Tauris, 1989), 57

5. Sufis performing the *dhikr* – 'remembrance' of God – near Omdurman, Sudan. Sufi rituals celebrate the divine in a purely disinterested way: the focus is on the absolute transcendence of God as distinct from His attributes, such as Mercy and Compassion

The famous mystic al-Hallaj (857–922) described his spiritual union with God in language ('I am the Truth') that the powers of the time saw as threatening to the authority of the caliph and the *'ulama*. He was crucified and burned, his ashes thrown into the river Tigris. The official reason for his execution was his teaching that the pilgrimage to Makka could be performed spiritually while staying at home. Despite occasional persecution, 'drunken' or ecstatic Sufism persisted alongside legalistic Islam. It animates Sufi-inspired poetry with constantly recurring images of divine love, challenging the conventional religiosity of what might be called 'the *'ulama* establishment'. Sufis often flirted with public obloquy and social danger, as if to prove that their love of God was wholly disinterested, uninfluenced by, indeed, contemptuous of, the social approval sought by the outwardly pious. Wine, forbidden to Muslims, became an emblem of spiritual ecstasy: homoeroticism (forbidden in theory, though in some cultures homosexuality was widely practised to preserve the 'honour' of women) is a recurring theme, where the divine is manifested in the beauty of beardless boys.

## A God beyond language

'In Arabic the word *wujud* is applied to God and to everything else as well...*Wujud* is not simply the fact of being or existing – the fact that something is there to be found. Rather, *wujud* is also the reality of finding, which is to say awareness, consciousness, understanding and knowledge.'

William Chittick on Ibn 'Arabi (2005)

'The cosmos has received nothing from the Real but *wujud*, and *wujud* is nothing other than the Real...So nothing remembers Him but something that has been given *wujud*, for there is nothing else...The cosmos stays in non-existence according to its root, though its properties become manifest in the *wujud* of the Real."

Ibn 'Arabi (1165–1240) *al-futuhat al-makiya* ('The Meccan Openings'), tr. William Chittick

> 'He is too sacred to have a likeness or similitude, for there cannot be a second to that absolute, innermost ipseity of things. He is beyond perception and beyond imagination and higher than that which can be comprehended or exemplified.'
>
> Mullah Sadra

Sufis sometimes derided the intellectual approach to the understanding of *tawhid* adopted by Isma'ilis and other neoplatonists, but in the writings of Ibn 'Arabi (1165–1240), whom many regard as the greatest of Sufi masters, the two approaches are fused. Ibn 'Arabi is sometimes accused of pantheism for his statement that 'nothing exists except Allah'. However, his system makes a categorical distinction between God's essence, which cannot be known or experienced by the mystic, and the level of unicity to which the mystic can aspire through the revelation of God's names. The 'inner reality' of Muhammad is identified with the First or Universal Intellect of the Neoplatonic system, deemed to have existed from all eternity, and with the Perfect Man of Sufi terminology – the microcosmic being through whom God contemplates himself, as in a mirror. Ibn Arabi could thus be described as a 'mystical humanist' for 'in a very real way [his] man is somehow God (in a sense that he is one with God like all things) and God is simply somehow man', though God is also much more than that. Ibn 'Arabi's system has been described as the 'ultimate theological semiosis in Islamic thought: everything signifies, and everything signifies only the One Reality, God'.

## Sufism and Shi'ism

The Sufi masters, renowned for their spirituality, became known as 'friends' (*walis*) of God, a term sometimes translated as 'saints', though as there is no church in Islam there are no formal processes of canonization. The intercessionary powers attributed to God's Friends endow them with the religious authority that leads to the creation of the Sufi orders (see Chapter 6). Inevitably there is considerable overlapping between the spiritual authority of the Imams and that of the Friends. Indeed, according to the Shi'i version of the declaration of faith, *There is no god but God, Muhammad is the Messenger of God,* 'Ali *is the Friend of God.* Just as 'Ali follows immediately after Muhammad in the chain of authorities through which some Sufi orders trace their respective rules, so the founders of Sufi orders are granted the same powers of interpretation into the esoteric meanings of scripture the Shi'a reserve for their Imams. Like the Imams, only the 'friends' are credited with fully understanding the Quran. Both Sufism and Shi'ism infuse the law with spiritual meanings; both endow their leaders with a measure of supernatural authority; both seek to establish avenues to illumination inspired by love of God rather than fear of punishment.

## Shi'ism and Iran

Iran has been a Shi'i state since the 16th century when Shah Isma'il, founder of the Safavid dynasty (1501–1722), persuaded a group of Turcoman nomads that he was the Hidden Imam and launched a successful invasion. The Safavid rulers and their later successors, the Qajars, eventually retreated from these claims, allowing a parallel system to develop in which the Shi'i *'ulama* acquired a considerable degree of autonomy. Under the Safavids, the synthesis of Neoplatonism and Sufi gnosis reached a further stage in the work of Mulla Sadra of Shiraz (1572–1641). Drawing on the illuminationist philosophy of al-Suhrawardi (d. 1191), Mulla Sadra believed that the divine light of knowledge flowed down through an unbroken chain from Adam, the first prophet, through the Greek philosophers (including Empedocles, Pythagoras, Socrates, Plato, Aristotle, and Plotinus), through Muhammad, the Imams and the Sufi masters, notably Ibn 'Arabi. His system admits no contradiction between free will and determinism, the God of philosophy and that of the Quran. Rational arguments are buttressed by intuitive, subjective experience in Mulla Sadra's scheme. However, scholars are far from unanimous about how successful he was in reconciling the two.

### The glory of *tawhid*

'The world view of *tawhid* is backed by the force of logic, science and reason. In every particle of the universe, there are indications of the existence of a wise, omniscient God; every tree leaf is a compendium of knowledge of the solicitous Lord.

The world view of *tawhid* gives meaning, spirit and aim to life because it sets man on the course of perfection that stops at no determinate limit but leads ever onward.

The world view of *tawhid* has a magnetic attraction; it imparts joy and confidence to man; it presents sublime and sacred aims; and it leads individuals to be self-sacrificing.

The world view of *tawhid* is the only world view in which individuals' mutual commitment and responsibility find meaning, Just as it is the only world view that saves man from falling into the terrible valley of belief in futility and worship of nothingness.'

Ayatullah Murtaza Mutahhari, *Fundamentals of Islamic Thought: God, Man and the Universe*, tr. R. Campbell (Berkeley, California: Mizan Press, 1985), 74

Despite the opposition of some of the *'ulama*, philosophical speculation has never been extinguished in the Shi'a tradition. The appearance of modernist ideas involved less of a disjunction of tradition than among the Sunnis. As deputies of the Hidden Imam the mullahs exercise the right of *ijtihad* – independent interpretation of the Shari'a – in contrast to most of their Sunni counterparts, who until recently tended to be bound by *taqlid* – 'imitation' of precedents applied by their predecessors. Mulla Sadra remains an important influence on such modern Shi'i clerical thinkers as Muhammad Hussein al-Tabatabai and Murtaza Mutahhari, as well as on lay thinkers such as 'Ali Shariati and Seyyed Hossein Nasr.

The authority of the Shi'i clergy is reinforced by the considerable wealth they dispose of as trustees of the numerous Shi'i shrines, recipients of religious taxes such as *zakat* and *khums*, and the corporate owners of urban and agricultural estates (for example, a religious endowment administered by the clergy owns more than half of Mashhad, Iran's eastern regional capital, a city of more than two million people). Prior to 1979, they had a long history of defiance to the state. In 1890 they launched a nation-wide boycott of all tobacco goods in protest against the granting of a royal monopoly to an Englishman, forcing the Shah into a humiliating retreat. This triumph led directly to constitutional revolution in 1905–6, in which the clergy played a leading, if ambivalent, part, with some of them seeking formal restrictions on the powers of the Shah while others strongly opposed a 'Western-style' constitution.

As befits *mujtahids* with the right of independent interpretation, the Shi'i clergy share a common culture, but they do not speak with one voice. To become a *mujtahid* a student must complete a course in theological studies before receiving written authorization to interpret the law. Having passed this stage he is given the honorary title *hujjat-al-islam* ('proof of Islam'). From the ranks of the *mujtahids*, of whom there are several hundreds, an internal consensus promotes those who have achieved eminence and seniority to the rank of *ayatallah* ('sign of God'). From the ranks of ayatollahs, who will already have their own followings among the theological students, five or six are chosen to become the Grand Ayatollahs who act as 'models to be imitated' (*marja's al-taqlid*). In theory every Shi'a person, whether clergy or laity, chooses one *marja'* as his or her religious guide. Given that *marjas* do not always agree with each other on matters of law or politics, the system allows for considerable diversity in theory, if not in the circumstances where senior clerics have come to exercise political power.

The historical independence of the Shi'i *'ulama* was favoured by the fact that two of the most important shrines and centres of Shi'i

**6. Demonstrations following the departure of Shah Mohammed Reza Pahlavi, 20 January 1979. Only a few months previously, US President Jimmy Carter described Iran as an 'island of stability' in the Middle East. The mass protests drew heavily on Shi'i themes of martyrdom and sacrifice**

learning, Karbala (the place of Hussein's martyrdom) and Najaf (mausoleum of 'Ali) lie outside Iran's borders, in the former Ottoman territory of Iraq. The Ottoman rulers were happy to encourage the political independence of the Shi'i clergy *vis-à-vis* their political rivals, the Persian shahs, provided they did not threaten their own interests. The tradition was maintained under the Ottoman Empire's successor-state Iraq which, despite having a population that is at least 55% Shi'i, had a government that remained firmly under Sunni control. In 1963, after mounting a vociferous campaign of opposition to the pro-Western Shah Mohammed Reza Pahlavi's social and agricultural reforms, a senior clergyman from Qum, Ayatollah Ruhallah Khomeini was expelled to Iraq and settled in Najaf. Here, under the benign sufferance of the Iraqi leader Saddam Hussein who had his own quarrels with the Shah, Khomeini was free to preach his doctrine of *Vilayet-e Faqih* (the 'governance of the jurist'). This was in effect an argument that in the absence of the Imam the *'ulama* had the right, if not the duty, to seize power – following the example of Imam Hussein rather than his elder brother Hasan. Photocopies and audio-cassettes of Khomeini's lectures were smuggled into Iran and widely disseminated among the population. In 1978, on the recommendation of the US Secretary of State Henry Kissinger, who tried to patch up the differences between Iran and Iraq, Khomeini was expelled. He chose to settle near Paris where, by astute manipulation of the international media, he was able to present himself as the Leader in Exile (while secretly engaging in correspondence with the Shah). Unusually for a Shi'i Ayatollah, he allowed himself to be referred to by the title Imam – a title normally reserved for the Twelve holy Imams in succession to the Prophet. While never explicitly claiming to be the Hidden Imam, his informal use of the title and his astute exploitation of the expectations surrounding it undoubtedly furthered his cause. When, in February 1979, following the Shah's departure, Khomeini flew to Tehran, two million people turned up at the airport to greet him. As one of Khomeini's leading opponents, the conservative Ayatollah Shariatmadari, observed: 'No one expected the Hidden Imam to arrive in a Jumbo Jet!'

Khomeini's dominance over the Iranian political scene until his death in 1989 (which saw equally extravagant scenes of mourning, the Imam, as it were, having chosen to go back into hiding) gave the false impression that he spoke for the Iranian clergy as a whole. In fact, two of his most vociferous opponents, the Ayatollahs Shariatmadari (d. 1986) and the popular 'left-wing' Taleqani (d. September 1979), came from the ranks of the senior clergy. His successor as supreme guide, 'Ali Khamenei, was chosen for his political rather than his religious qualifications. His status as a *marja* or Grand Ayatollah (as required by the Constitution) was disputed by other *marjas* including the Mohammed Shirazi (1928–2001) and Hossein-'Ali Montazeri (1922–2009), who was passed over for the leadership after criticizing the regime's human rights abuses and Khomeini's *fatwa* stating that the British author

Salman Rushdie should be killed. Khamenei's control over numerous state bodies, including the fascist-style Basij militias, enabled him to suppress the reformist protests that erupted in Tehran and other cities after the disputed presidential contest of 2009, when the hard-line President Mahmoud Ahmadinejad was elected for a second term. Khamenei and Ahmadinejad have reversed many of the liberalizing reforms begun under the presidency of Muhammad Khatami, who had come to power in a landslide victory in 1997. Khamenei's reactionary activism may be contrasted with the reluctance of Grand Ayatollah 'Ali al-Sistani in neighbouring Iraq to engage in politics directly. Sistani endorsed the democratic reforms instituted in the wake of the 2003 US-led invasion that overthrew the Ba'athist regime of Saddam Hussein, urging all Iraqis, especially women, to vote, and he demanded that Iraqi Shi'a refrain from retaliating against the wave of sectarian killings, sponsored by al-Qaeda and Wahhabi elements in Saudi Arabia, that occurred in the wake of the invasion. With his immense prestige as the world's pre-eminent Shi'a cleric, Sistani may have been a restraining influence on the radical forces of Shi'ism led by Muqtada al-Sadr, more than forty years his junior, whose father Grand Ayatollah Baqir al-Sadr had been executed by the regime of Saddam Hussein. By urging his followers to lay down their arms and enter the political process, al-Sadr made a significant contribution to the survival of Iraq as a democracy.

Paradoxically, the activity of America and its principal ally Israel had served to strengthen Shi'i political forces that had previously been repressed. In Lebanon, the Shi'i Hizbollah movement that emerged in the wake of Israeli incursions into the southern part of the country became the country's leading political force, while in Bahrain, where a Shi'i majority had long languished under the rule of a minority Sunni regime, protestors demanding civil rights and a more equitable distribution of the country's wealth were brutally suppressed by Sunni troops 'bussed' in from Saudi Arabia, Jordan, and Pakistan. The Saudi dynasty, whose legitimacy depends on the support of virulently anti-Shi'a Wahhabi clerics, was clearly alarmed that Shi'a unrest would spread to the oil-bearing region around Dhahran, where Shi'a are a local majority. Given the toxic combination of local conflicts and the financial leverage disposed by wealthy Sunni paymasters in Arabia and the Gulf, the sectarian unrest and hatred has been exported to Central and South Asia. In Afghanistan, before its overthrow by US armed forces in 2002, the Salafist Taliban regime had launched genocidal attacks on the Shi'i Hazaras, bringing the country to the brink of war with Iran. In Pakistan, Sunni terrorist groups inspired by Salafist propaganda have inflicted murderous attacks on Shi'a in schools and mosques and villages. With globalization and modern weaponry, a conflict originating in a dispute about inheritance more than fourteen centuries ago retains its power to wreak havoc and misery.

# Chapter 4
# The Shariʿa and its consequences

## Introduction

Just as there is no doctrine of divine incarnation in Islam, so there is no church, no separate institution or body distinct from the rest of society charged with the task of conveying God's will, or the Prophet's teachings, to the ordinary believer. In Islam, 'God has not revealed Himself and His nature, but rather His law'. The term 'Shariʿa' applies to much more than law in the strictly legal sense. It includes the details of ritual, as well as a whole range of customs and manners, although local customary laws are also recognized. Shariʿa means literally 'the way to a watering place': the Quranic use of the term suggestively combines the notions of a vital means of sustenance in this world and access to the divine realm of the world to come. The law is there both for the purpose of upholding the good of society and for helping human beings attain salvation. Interpretations of the law may vary in accordance with time and place, but the Shariʿa itself is considered to be a timeless manifestation of the will of God, subject neither to history nor circumstance.

The development of the Shariʿa law was primarily the result of the historic conditions prevailing during Islam's three formative centuries. Coins dating from the reign of ʿAbd al-Malik and some early ʿAbbasid rulers contain the inscription *khalifat Allah* (God's deputy or vice-regent): the early caliphs evidently saw themselves as the divinely appointed fountainheads of law. They based their legal rulings on the Quran, the so-called *Sunna* of local practice, and decisions based – like those of the Shi'i Imam – on their own divinely inspired insights. Only later did the concept of *Sunna* come to be applied exclusively to deeds or sayings of the Prophet, as subsequently recorded in the *hadith* literature. (For example, the Caliph 'Umar changed the penalty for adultery from the 100 lashes given in the Quran to stoning – a decision later supported by reference to various *hadiths* attributed to the Prophet.) In later times, the title *khalifat rasul Allah* (deputy of the Messenger of God) came into use, indicating that the Caliph was now seen in a less elevated capacity as the Prophet's Successor. And it is the Prophet whose custom or *Sunna* looms increasingly large as the primary source of law. The change of nomenclature coincided with the failure of the *mihna*, or 'inquisition', which saw the end of the Caliph's attempts to fuse religious and political leadership in his person.

The civil wars and leadership struggles following Muhammad's death eventually limited the Caliph's power and limited his governance, leaving no source of authority uncontested save that of the Quran and the Prophet's precepts, embodied in the burgeoning corpus of *hadiths*. Indeed, the manner in which the Prophet's Sunna eclipses that of the caliphs, as well as that of his Companions and their Successors, closely parallels the development of the Shari'a itself. Local or regional 'living' traditions based on more or less pragmatic judicial decisions of Muslim commanders and the judges they appoint are replaced by more systematic efforts to determine the Will of God, as revealed in the Quran and *hadith*. The juristic literature through which the Shari'a, God's law or way is elaborated and made explicit is known as *fiqh*, 'knowledge' or 'understanding' (a term often translated by the more technical 'jurisprudence'). Its four roots (*usul*), in order of precedence, are the Quran, the Prophet's *Sunna* (as revealed through the *hadith* literature), *ijma'* or consensus, and *qiyas* (analogical reasoning).

## The roots of Islamic law

### 1. Quran

As the direct and unmediated Word of God, the Quran is the primary source of law in Islam. In the broadest sense, the whole of the Quran is law for Muslims. God proclaims himself in a Book, every single verse of which can be perceived as a divine command. Only a small proportion, however – about 10% of the Quran's 6,000 verses – contains injunctions that can be converted into positive religious or legal requirements. Most of these occur in passages dating from the Madinese period when the Prophet was actively engaged in lawmaking. There are prohibitions on certain foods (pork, carrion, wine, animals slaughtered in pagan ceremonies), a number of legal rules concerning family law (marriage, divorce, and inheritance), criminal law (the *hudud* crimes, including penalties of highway robbery, illicit sexual activity, slander, and wine drinking), rules about witnesses, and commercial regulations including the ban on *riba* (usury) and forms of contracts. None of these rules is wholly free from ambiguities, and lawyers who relied exclusively on the Quran for legislative material would soon find themselves engaged in 'endless debate about whether some verses have been abrogated by others, as most Muslims believe; and if so, which verses were abrogated by which'.

### A moral universe

'The Quran is an unparalleled window into the moral universe. It is a source of knowledge in the way that the entire corpus of legal precedent is for the common law tradition: not so much as an index of possible rulings as a quarry in which the astute inquirer can hope to find the building blocks for a morally valid, and therefore, true system of ethics ... The *hadith*-reports, considered as a whole, contain the *sunna* of the Prophet, which is not simply a record of the Prophetic doings but of the Prophet's significant, exemplary acts, non-acts, and sayings. The Quran's integrity was guaranteed by its miraculous inimitability and plural transmission; the prophetic *sunna* was vouched for by the immaculate protection (*isma*) of the Prophet, Quranic attestation, and plural transmission. What is noteworthy is that, except in broad outline, the *sunna* was not a mere catalog of model behaviour to be emulated, but rather a collection of data which required assessment and application in an appropriate context. A life lived totally in accord with the Moral becomes a window into moral knowledge. The Prophet is thus, for the practitioner of *fiqh*, not really a model but a normative case, not so much a person as a principle.'

Kevin Reinhart, 'Islamic Law as Islamic Ethics', *Journal of Religious Ethics*, 11/2 (Fall 1983), 189, 190

## 2. *Sunna*

The Prophet's custom as recorded in the *hadith* literature contains a much larger quantity of legal material than the Quran, based in many cases on the Prophet's own legal judgments. Although Western scholars and some Muslim modernists (like some of the early authorities) have questioned the authenticity of many of these *hadiths*, the *Sunna* remains for the vast majority of Muslims the uncontested and uncontestable second root of divine law. The *Sunna*, however, is very far from being self-explanatory: some *hadiths* will contradict others, experts will disagree about which are strong and which are weak, and without the two additional 'roots' of law – *ijma'* (consensus) and *qiyas* (analogical reasoning) – coherent legal decision-making would be impossible.

## 3. Ijma'

In the first centuries after the Muslim conquest, the scholars who interpreted the law in the different urban centres relied on their own consensus and that of their illustrious predecessors to reach agreement over which *hadiths* should be accepted and which rejected as sources of law. The idea that *ijma'* should be regarded as a 'root' of jurisprudence was enshrined in a hadith of the Prophet: 'My community will never agree upon an error.' As Muslims would come to see it, *ijma'* was active in the earliest days of Islam when the memory of the Prophet's example was still alive and the community small and culturally homogeneous enough to engage in common practice. Thus the jurist Muhammad b. al-Hasan al-Shaibani (749–805), commenting on a particular legal decision states: 'Whatever the Muslims see as good is good with God, and whatever the Muslims see as bad is bad with God.' For example, circumcision (male and in some areas female) became normative if not universal though it had no sanction other than Arab custom. *Hadiths* accepted and followed by this early consensus included rulings of the Companions and their Successors as well as those of the Prophet himself. Had Islamic legal development continued along these lines it is probable that a proliferation of regional sects, each claiming for itself universal status, would have resulted. The great Palestinian jurist al-Shafi'i devoted his career to standardizing the law, making sure that the most important *hadiths* were traced directly to the Prophet. Whereas earlier *hadiths* might contradict each other, the oral law, like the written law embodied in the Quran, was now believed to come directly from God through the Prophet, and must therefore be free from inconsistencies. The new idea of *ijma'* that crystallized around this doctrine bore the imprint of the consensus of the community as distinct from that of the legal scholars. The Prophet's imprimatur on these legal traditions guaranteed wide if not universal public acceptability. It has been suggested, however, that the creativity and adaptability present during the era of the 'living schools' was accordingly diminished.

## Five schools of jurisprudence

In addition to Muhammad ibn Idris al-Shafi'i (767–820) the four legal schools of Sunni Islam are named after Abu Hanifa (699–767) an Iraqi of Persian extraction, Malik ibn Anas al-Asbahi (713–795) an Arab of Yemeni descent who spent the whole of his life in Medina, leaving it but once to perform the pilgrimage, and Ahmad Ibn Hanbal (780–855) an uncompromising hadith-collector and traditionist who eschewed *ijma'* and used reasoning by analogy only when the Quran, the hadiths and legal rulings of Companions had been exhausted. The Shi'a have their own school of law, the Ja'fari school, named after the Sixth Imam, Ja'far al Sadiq (see Chapter 4), in which *hadiths* of 'Ali and the Imams feature prominently alongside those of the Prophet.

Of the four Sunni schools the Hanafi became the most influential, being the official school of the 'Abbasid caliphs and later of the Ottoman sultans. Today, it is the dominant school in religious and family law among the Muslims of the Balkans, Transcaucasia, Afghanistan, Pakistan, India, the central Asian republics, and China. The Maliki school was represented in the Hijaz and spread to the Gulf as well as to Upper Egypt and the Sudan, Andalusia, and north-west Africa, so that it is now the dominant school in Morocco, Algeria, Tunisia, and Libya. The Shafi'i school is less widely represented than the Hanafi in the Middle East – not least because the Hanafi school displaced it in Egypt after the Ottoman conquest in 1517. Today, its followers are to be found mainly in the rural parts of Egypt, Palestine, Jordan, the coastlands of Yemen, and among populations in Pakistan, India, and Indonesia, the world's most populous Muslim country.

## 4. *Qiyas*

The fourth of the classical 'roots of jurisprudence' is a form of analogical and syllogistic reasoning similar to the Talmudic *heqqes* from which, some argue, the word has been derived. In principle, it involved the systematic application of logic to situations not explicitly mentioned in the Quran or *hadith*. During the formative period of Islamic law, its application was controversial, and some jurists argued against it on the ground that it imputed inadequacy to the Prophet and the Holy Quran. Its defenders, however, cited a *hadith* according to which the Prophet sent one of his Companions, Muadh ibn Jabal, to be a judge in Yemen. Before he departed, the Prophet subjected him to a brief interrogation:

> 'How will you reach a judgment when a question arises?'
> 'According to the word of God', replied Muadh.
> 'And if you find no solution in the word of God?'
> 'Then according to the *sunna* of the Messenger of God.'
> 'And if you find no solution in the *sunna* of the Messenger of God nor in the Word?'
> 'Then I shall take a decision according to my own opinion (*rayi*).'
> The Prophet was pleased with this answer. He slapped Muadh on the chest, saying 'Praise be to God who has led the Messenger of God to an answer that pleased him'.

The clearest examples of the use of analogical or syllogistic reasoning involves alcoholic drinks. While some jurists would argue that only fermented products of the date-palm and vine are forbidden, others, basing their judgements on *qiyas*, would insist that all alcoholic drinks are forbidden, since the effective cause or common denominator (*'illa*) behind the prohibition was the same in each case: 'All intoxicating drinks count as grape-wine. Vodka is an intoxicating drink. Therefore vodka is forbidden.'

## Religious and social duties

The record of human understanding of the divine will was collated in vast compendia known as the books of *fiqh*. These books are not legal codes, but they do offer guidance for judges. The typical *fiqh* manual is divided into religious and social duties (*'ibadat* and *mu'amalat*). The section on *'ibadat* will focus primarily on the Five *Rukns* or 'Pillars' (see Appendix). It will have detailed prescriptions about ablutions, the times and exact performance of prayer both privately and on Friday, the Day of Congregation; *zakat* (compulsory charity); the Ramadan fast, and the pilgrimage to Makka.

*Mu'amalat* are the laws governing human relationships; in their modern application they are largely confined to questions of personal status, marriage, and inheritance as well as prohibitions on forbidden substances such as pork or wine. They also include political matters such as the theory of the caliphate which in classical times fell within the active purview of the Shari'a.

## *Ijtihad*: the struggle for truth

Legal reasoning by analogy and syllogism was one aspect of the interpretative effort (*ijtihad*) needed to fathom the law as revealed by God and his Prophet. The word *ijtihad* shares the same root as *jihad* ('struggle') – a term usually translated as 'holy war'. The jurist must exhaust himself intellectually in order to determine the details of God's command. *Ijtihad*, in the words of one authority, involves 'the total expenditure of effort in the search for an opinion as to any legal rule in such a manner that the individual senses (within himself) an inability to expend further effort'. The goal is not law making, but *fiqh* – understanding or knowledge of a law deemed to exist already.

The Shari'a is assumed to be divine, co-eternal with God, although some scholars will dispute this usage. *Fiqh*, by contrast, is the product of human endeavour. The *faqih* – one who practises *fiqh* – is a legal specialist who seeks through exercising *ijtihad* to reach conclusions about the Shari'a, to determine the implications of God's commands in particular instances. If he is unable to exercise *ijtihad*, he should use another method known as *taqlid* – the imitation of a recognized *mujtahid*. For if everyone exercised personal *ijtihad*, the result would be chaos. In the course of time the jurists became increasingly reluctant to practise *ijtihad*, preferring to rely on *taqlid*. Juridical loyalties crystallized around the four leading figures credited with founding the four main legal schools (*madhhabs*) of Sunni Islam.

The differences between the four legal schools are mainly confined to questions such as marriage and guardianship, with the Hanafis taking a more liberal view of female rights than the Malikis. Legal differences between the Sunni schools and Shi'i Ja'fari school are not very great. There are small differences in the ritual of prayer. The most significant are in the laws of inheritance and in an institution known as *mut'a* (Persian *sigheh*) or temporary marriage (see Chapter 5). Although jurists from all schools with the exception of the Hanbalis continued to exercise *ijtihad* for many centuries, the doctrine emerged that the 'gates of *ijtihad*' had been closed after the third Muslim century. Recent scholarship, however, suggests that the gates were never closed completely, and that famous *mujtahids* in the Sunni tradition continued to practise at least until the 16th century CE.

In Shi'i jurisprudence the 'gates of *ijtihad*' are generally assumed to have remained open. Senior Shi'i *'ulama* known by the title of hujjat al-Islam ('proof of Islam') or Ayatullah ('sign of God') are all *mujtahids* – individual interpreters of the law. Every believing Shi'i is supposed to place him or herself under the guidance of a *mujtahid* who acts as a 'source of imitation' (*marja- i- taqlid* in Persian). The Shi'i *'ulama* are the recipients of religious taxes (*zakat* and *khums*) and historically this has given them more independence of government than their Sunni counterparts. The autonomy of the religious establishment *vis-à-vis* the state makes it an 'estate' comparable to the Christian clergy or Buddhist Sangha. The independent network of mosques allied to the traditional business sector (the 'bazaar') enabled the Iranian religious establishment to take power through its political wing, the Islamic Republican Party, during the events that accompanied the collapse of the Pahlavi dynasty in the winter of 1978–9 (see Chapter 6).

The intellectual and hermeneutical flexibility of the Shi'i *'ulama* have given them the edge over their Sunni counterparts in adapting the law to contemporary circumstances. Where Sunni Islamists have actively sought political power, it has often been freelancers or religious auto-didacts who have made the running. Where scholarly-trained individuals, such as Shaikh 'Ali Ben Hadj of Algeria or Shaikh 'Umar 'Abd al-Rahman of Egypt, have become involved in political or terrorist activity, it has not been in their capacities as members of the religious establishment, but rather as charismatic individuals. In the Sunni tradition the *fiqh* began to calcify within its own intellectual sphere, becoming increasingly divorced from the realities of the vast and diverse domains acquired by Muhammad's successors. Al-Shafi'i's insistence – adopted by the other *madhhabs* – on pinning as many legal rulings as possible to the Prophet's example ensured a remarkable degree of uniformity, though local and regional customs inevitably persisted – often under the guise of *hadiths* of doubtful authenticity. This is not to say, however, that the system was monolithic. There remained considerable diversity within the corpus of Islamic jurisprudence as it developed, the variations justified by reference to another important hadith: 'The differences between the learned of my community are a blessing from God.'

## The Shari'a: an all-encompassing ideal

The books of *fiqh* divide human conduct into five categories which cover everything 'from murder to social etiquette, and from incest to the rules of religious retreat'. The categories in the varied terminology of the jurists comprise the things that are commanded, recommended, left legally indifferent, disapproved of, and forbidden. The formulation involved the explicit rejection of the view advocated by the Mu'tazila that the moral world could be divided into the bipolar categories of good and evil. The fivefold system represents the compromise made in the first two centuries between the moral perfectionism of early Muslim communities such as the Kharijis, and the demands of an expanding Islamic community that aimed to be inclusive and universal.

In principle, this remarkably comprehensive scheme allows no ultimate distinction between religion and morality, law and ethics. All are seen as proceeding directly from the command of God, though there is room for humans to argue about the details. Only God can judge the extent to which an individual's activities conform to the jurists' schema. Law in the narrower sense is restricted to dealing with those activities that are explicitly forbidden (*haram*) or to adjudicating between competing claims of individuals.

Western legal historians tend to argue that the Shari'a developed as an ideal system of law divorced from practice. The mainly oral procedure and high standards of proof – though admirable for protecting the rights of accused persons in relatively small communities such as the Prophet's Medina – were less appropriate in the expanding cosmopolitan societies of the Arab empire. Strictures against *riba* (lending and borrowing at fixed rates of interest) were widely evaded by legal devices, making whole areas of commercial law impossible to enforce. As a consequence the administration of criminal justice was never fully entrusted to the *qadis*. The *qadi* courts were supplemented by those of the police, while the *muhtasib*, the Inspector of Markets – a lineal descendant of the Byzantine *agronamos* – took a vast range of commercial practice under his wing. Where they found the Shari'a rules inadequate, inappropriate, or limiting the rulers added their own supplementary decrees and enforced laws other than the Shari'a in the *mazalim* courts, the rulers' Courts of Complaints.

## Five categories of behaviour

The classical lawbooks divide all human behaviour into five categories:

1. Required, obligatory (*wajib* or *fard*) 'for the neglect of which one ought to be punished (both in this world and in the hereafter) and for the doing of which one is rewarded'. Obligations are divided into *fard 'ain*, individual duties, such as prayer, alms giving and fasting; and *fard kifaya*, collective duties, such as attendance at funeral prayers or participation in the jihad or holy war.

2. Proscribed or prohibited (*mahzur*, *haram*), acts 'for the performance of which there is punishment and (according to most authorities) for the avoidance of which there is reward'. The punishment is usually inflicted in this world according to Islamic law. Categories include certain types of theft, illicit sexual activity, wine drinking – the so-called *hudud* offences – for which specific penalties are prescribed in the Quran. The rewards for abstention are presumed to be in paradise.

3. Recommended (*mandub*, *masnun*, *mustahabb*, *sunna*): acts that are commendable but not required, 'for the doing of which there is reward, but for the neglect of which there is no punishment'. They include charitable acts such as the manumission of slaves, supererogatory prayers and fasts, pious deeds of all varieties.

4. Discouraged or odious (*makruh*), 'acts for the doing of which there is no punishment, but for the avoidance of which there is reward'. There is wide disagreement about this category but some authorities would include divorce, permitted by unilateral male declaration, but disapproved of by the Prophet.

5. Permitted but morally indifferent (*jaiz*, *mubah*), 'acts for the performance or avoidance of which there is neither reward nor punishment'.

### The judge's role

An American legal anthropologist who attended sessions of a Moroccan Shari'a court over several years observed:

'Rather than being aimed simply at the invocation of state or religious power... the aim of the *qadi* is to put people back in the position of being able to negotiate their own permissible relationships without predetermining just what the outcome of those negotiations ought to be... Even the social interest is conceptualized in terms of maintaining private interaction: what is good for the individual is good for society. What is missing, until at least the beginning of western influence, is the institutionalization of the public as an entity whose interests might be assessed like those of a person. In the absence of the idea that corporate entities might constitute jural personalities the social interest enters the law as a localized interpretation of the legal status of particular named persons and their highly personalized acts.'

Lawrence Rosen, *The Anthropology of Justice: Law as Culture in Islamic Society* (Cambridge: Cambridge University Press, 1989), 17, 49

## The Shari'a and Muslim societies

By defining correct behaviour or orthopraxy at the social level, the Shari'a has left its distinctive imprint on a way of living that has evolved over time and varies from one country to another in accordance with local custom.

As well as sanctioning sexual inequality (see Chapter 5), the laws of inheritance prevented concentrations of wealth among individuals, as estates had to be divided according to the provisions of the Shari'a which limits the amount a single heir may inherit while favouring a multiplicity of claims by agnatic kin (relatives in the male line). Although these provisions could be evaded by the creation of family trusts (*awqaf*),

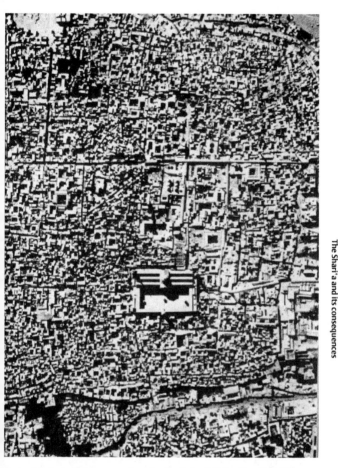

7. Aerial view of Damascus showing the labyrinthine density of the streets in the old city. In the absence of a formally constituted public domain, the streets were constantly subject to private encroachments

endowments from which the founders' families could draw incomes in perpetuity, such provisions may have worked against the productive use of capital for commercial and industrial purposes.

The Shari'a, both in theory and practice, was uncompromisingly individualistic. The absence of the concept of church – the mystical 'body of Christ' that stood between the individual Christian and God through which alone salvation was possible – militated against the creation of institutions such as the medieval Western city or trading company where the group interest transcended that of the individual. The Shari'a recognized no corporate entities which could be treated as persons in law. The purpose of the law, apart from enforcing God's commands, was to regulate the affairs of men. One consequence of the absence of the concept of jural personality or legal personhood of groups may be seen in the proliferating alleyways of many pre-modern Middle East cities, where private territory – cafés, workshops, stalls, and so forth – constantly encroaches on public space. The public domain, it is presumed, is simply the sum of its private components, not a separate entity requiring legal protection. The positive result is a law that is primarily directed at social self-regulation. The Muslim judge, like the ancient hadith collector, must be above all a judge of persons. In the words of a Saudi Arabian scholar, he must have 'an acute sense of observation: for example just by looking at a suspect he should be able to tell what the man has concealed in his testimony'. In traditional Muslim societies, the 'science of men' administered by the judge provided the connecting link between divine justice and the human environment in which it was supposed to operate. The idealism of the Shari'a was mitigated by a humane and humanistic pragmatism.

## Shari'a as a field of moral inquiry, not applied ethics

The term Shari'a is often used in public discourse as if it is synonymous with Islam itself, as the totality of obligations of Muslims both in the private, personal religious sense and in social, political and legal norms and institutions. In fact the Shari'a is only the door and passageway into being Muslim and does not exhaust the possibilities of human knowledge and lived experience of Islam... It should also be emphasized that any conception of Shari'a is necessarily and always derived from human interpretation of the Quran and the Sunna, reflecting what fallible human beings are able to comprehend and seek to comply with given the limitations of their own specific historical context.

As a Muslim, I need a secular state in order to live in accordance with the Shari'a out of my own genuine conviction and free choice, personally and in community with other Muslims, which is the only valid and legitimate way of being a Muslim. Belief in Islam, or an other religion, logically requires the possibility of disbelief, because belief has no value if it is coerced.

Abdullahi Ahmed An-Na'im, *Islam and the Secular State* (2008), 291, 268

A negative consequence of the Shari'a approach to law has been the lack of legitimacy accorded the public interest in the form of city, state, or any other institution standing between the individual and God. Corruption is endemic in many societies, and it would be grossly unfair to target Muslim societies as being uniquely prone to bribery, graft, and the private misappropriation of public funds. Patrimonialism – the confusion of private and public realms – is rife in much of the world beyond the regions that were part of Western Christendom. Nevertheless, a culture informed by the absence of institutional boundaries between the public and private spheres may be more vulnerable to such abuses than one where the boundaries are rigorously upheld by law. In Western societies, these boundaries are part of the historical residue of medieval Christendom, with its separate distribution of powers between church and state. 'Family values' including those of the extended kinship group are fundamental to Shari'a and, where family values predominate, the state is vulnerable to manipulation by powerful family networks. Yet the idealism implicit in the Shari'a, the utopian expectations it engenders, militates against the constitutional limitation of power. It is pessimism about human nature (a by-product, arguably, of the Christian doctrine of original sin) that leads to the liberal perception that all power corrupts, and that constitutional limitations must be placed on its exercise. This personalized or individualized nature of the Shari'a has not merely given its application an intimate and personal character – a character that is, arguably, reinforced, by the application of public corporal punishments including flogging and execution, for certain categories of crime. It impeded economic, and hence, political development. The absence of a concept of legal personhood not only blurred the boundaries between private and public realms, it arguably prevented the emergence of the kind of corporate structures that enabled Western societies to develop a whole range of civil society institutions from universities to trading companies, trades unions to clubs. Moreover, as a recent study of Islamic economic history suggests, the combination of Islamic inheritance laws, which required the distribution of assets upon a merchant's death, and the absence of legal personhood, prevented Middle Eastern societies from competing successfully with European ones, once the latter had developed sophisticated corporate structures, as happened from the 18th century. This in effect made most Muslim societies ripe for the European take-over – such as the British occupation of Egypt – that occurred in the 19th century.

> By fragmenting the estates of successful merchants [the Shari'a] kept Islamic commercial partnerships small and short-lived; it also dampened pressures to develop complex enterprises. The consequent lack of organizational progress did not pose a major problem as long as no other region had modernized. However, it became a huge handicap for merchants operating under Islamic law as organizational advances in the West brought about larger and more durable enterprises.

In the view of some observers, the Shari'a's individualistic idealism traps the modern Islamist political discourse in what might be called a 'virtuous circle'. Rather than addressing systemic or institutional reform, modern Islamist reformers like Maududi have simply stressed a 'return' to the Shari'a, placing an excessive degree of emphasis on personal virtue. As the French scholar Olivier Roy points out, because the Islamist model is predicated on the belief in government by morally impeccable individuals who can be counted on to resist temptation, it does not generate institutions capable of functioning autonomously by means of structural checks and balances. The theory, as he sees it, is tautological: political institutions function only as a result of the virtue of those who run them, but virtue can become widespread only if society is already Islamic.

# Chapter 5
# Women and family

## Introduction

No subject is more fraught with controversy than the relation of women and Islam. On one side of the debate there exists the widespread perception that the faith oppresses and even persecutes women; at the other there are arguments about cultural authenticity, about the rights of women to assert themselves in ways that differ from the modes of female self-assertion current in non-Muslim societies. The issue is complicated by the interaction of history, religion, culture, and politics. Historically the patriarchal family and the extended networks of kinship connected with it have proved to be among the most durable social structures in Muslim societies, far more durable than structures built around professional association or class interest. The role of religion in sustaining these structures is not entirely clear. Islamic law privileges the family over other institutions: the laws of inheritance, favouring males over females, are written in the Quran along with other discriminatory provisions, such as the testamentary inferiority of females in certain court proceedings. The law, however, is not always a reliable guide to actual social practice: slavery and concubinage, widely practised in pre-colonial times, are also the subject of detailed legal provisions and though permitted under the Shari'a, both have disappeared (in theory if not always in practice) from Muslim societies. Unlike the *hijab*, or 'veil', they are not among the shibboleths insisted upon by today's Islamists.

Protection of the patriarchal family and the symbolic capital it holds in the shape of female chastity is deeply embedded in the semantics of Islam: the word *haram* (sacred, forbidden, taboo) shares the same root with *harim* – the part of the household reserved for women – and *mahram* – the kinship group to which a woman is forbidden sexually by law, and within which she is free to associate. The duality of the manifest and the hidden (*al-shahada/al-ghaib, al-zahir/al-batin*), fundamental to the Quranic approach to the divine, is suggestively linked in at least one passage to sexuality, with the female pudenda associated with the hidden aspect of deity. Restrictions on women are intimately bound up with notions of the sacred. As Michael Gilsenan has observed of village life in northern Lebanon, *sharaf*, 'the honour of person and family which is particularly identified with control of women's sexuality, is crucial to the public, social identity of men'. The same observation applies, *a fortiori*, in many other parts of the Muslim world. But an obsession with gender and status and its corollary, the assertion of masculine power through violence, is by no means exclusively Islamic. The same patriarchal assumptions are found in non-Muslim Mediterranean societies as well as others further afield. Conversely there are Muslim communities in West Africa and South-East Asia where matrilineal systems of ownership and inheritance predominate. All of this calls into question the view that Islamic texts and the values they enshrine are of themselves responsible for types of behaviour underpinning male supremacism. At the same time there can be no doubt that the public and symbolic role of women lies at the heart of the Islamist discourse. In one polemic after another Islamist writers contrast the virtuous Muslim woman with her Western or Westernized counterpart – naked, unchaste, and corrupt, a potent source of *fitna*, or strife.

## Women and the Shari'a

As with other politically charged issues in contemporary Islam, the debate surrounding the veil is fuelled by diverging perspectives upon an exemplary past. Traditionalists, most of them men, argue that the Prophet of Islam greatly improved the position of the Arabian women of his time, guaranteeing them basic rights in marriage that were denied to the women of the time of ignorance – the *jahiliya*. Makkan *suras* of the Quran refer with abhorrence to the custom of female infanticide and the neglect of widows and orphans. After Islam, women were given guaranteed rights of inheritance under the protective umbrella of the family. A woman's husband was obligated to provide for her and her children. Although polygyny (one man and a plurality of wives) was permitted, the man was limited to four wives, each of whom had to be treated equally. No spiritual inequality is implied. The Quran explicitly addresses itself to females as well as males, and morally women will be as answerable for their actions on the Day of Judgement as men.

### Spiritual equality

*Muslim men and Muslim women,*
*Believing men and believing women,*
*Devout men and devout women,*
*Sincere men and sincere women,*
*Patient men and patient women,*
*Humble men and humble women,*
*Charitable men and charitable women,*
*Fasting men and fasting women,*
*Men who guard their chastity, and women who*
*guard their chastity,*

That said, however, there are particular verses which testify to the
legal inferiority of women. A sister shares only half the portion of
her brothers under the Quranic laws of inheritance – the
assumption being that her husband will maintain her. A husband
may physically chastise a recalcitrant or disobedient wife as a final
resort when other measures have failed. In certain legal
proceedings a woman's testimony is only worth half that of a man:
it is assumed that she will be unfamiliar with business matters and
that she will need a friend to jog her memory. In the context of
7th-century Arabia these Quranic rubrics are not necessarily
incompatible with the argument that Islam substantially
improved the status of women, not least by improving their
security in marriage and property. Modern feminists wishing to
move beyond these positions, however, face a theological obstacle.
As the unalterable speech of God the Quran is deemed to be
non-negotiable: for the majority of Muslims, the spirit is firmly
anchored in the letter. To argue that modern conditions demand
an end to the Quran's discriminatory provisions is to challenge the
dogma that the text is fixed for eternity. Feminist writers are
forced by the logic of their position to de-couple the text from the
spirit in favour of a flexible doctrine that leads inevitably to the
recontextualization of Islam's holy book. The issue of women's
rights is inexorably caught up in the issue of modernism.

As modernists see it, the Quran was revealed at a specific time and
in a specific social context. Their task is to reinterpret the spirit of
its provisions in the light of modern realities. The difficulty facing
modernists is that those who take the text at face value, refusing to

## Male authority

*'Your women are your sowing field: approach your field whenever you please. Lay up good works for yourselves and fear God, and know that you shall surely meet Him. Proclaim glad tidings to the believers.'*

(Quran 2: 222)

*'Men are legally responsible for women, in as much as God has preferred some of you over others in bounty, and because of what they spend of their wealth. Thus virtuous women are obedient, and preserve their trusts, such as God wishes them to be preserved. And those you fear may rebel, admonish, and abandon them in their beds, and smack them. If they obey you, seek no other way against them. God is the Highest and Mightiest.'*

(Quran 4: 34)

'Whenever the Prophet (peace be on him) permitted a man to administer corporal punishment to his wife, he did so with reluctance, and continued to express his distaste for it. And even in cases where it is necessary, the Prophet (peace be on him) directed men not to hit across the face, nor to beat severely nor to use anything that might leave marks on the body.'

From Maududi's commentary on Quran 4: 34 in Sayyid Abul Ala Maududi, *Tafhim al-Quran*, tr. and ed. Zafar Ishaq Ansari (Leicester: Islamic Foundation, 1989), ii, 36

deconstruct it to suit current social trends or fashions, are often closer to its original meaning and purpose. One way out of this difficulty, adopted by the American translator Laleh Bakhtiar, is to challenge conventional meanings of particular words. She argues that the verb *daraba* used in the passage quoted above, normally translated as to 'hit' or 'spank', has a number of different root meanings, including to 'go away'. So in her reading, husbands of recalcitrant wives are simply enjoined to leave them. Other strategies involve adding modern ethical perspectives to the interpretation of Quranic verses. For example, the verses allowing polygyny require that each wife be treated equally. Traditionalists interpreted equality in legalistic terms: the right of each wife to her own household, to equality of material provision. Modernists undermine the whole institution by adding an emotional and psychological dimension to the notion of equality, arguing that since no man can be expected to be emotionally involved with all his wives equally, polygyny is effectively ruled out.

Similar arguments are deployed by modernists to rationalize the draconian punishments against unfaithful wives or individuals accused of illicit sexual activity (*zina*). Under the strict Quranic rules of evidence, the crime of *zina* must be attested by four independent adult male witnesses to the act itself. Since in the nature of things such a provision is almost impossible to satisfy, according to this argument sexual propriety is maintained in principle while intrusive social censoriousness is avoided. Thus Leila Badawi draws attention to legal interpretations that appear liberal by pre-modern standards: in the case of a deserted or widowed woman who becomes pregnant she may be protected by the legal fiction (*hila*) of the 'sleeping foetus', according to which a pregnancy can be accepted as lasting five or even seven years, while the child remains the legal heir of the dead or absent husband. An unmarried woman who becomes pregnant can resort to the fiction of the 'public bath'. Baths were traditionally opened on alternating days or hours for men and women, and a virgin, it was claimed, who visited the public baths after the men had just vacated them might inadvertently sit on a pool of semen thereby making herself pregnant.

## Two views of polygamy

*'Marry whoever pleases you among women – two, three or four; but if you fear you will not be fair to them all, then one only, or*

*else what you own as slaves. This would be closer to
impartiality.' 3)*

(Quran 4: 3)

'Some people who have been overwhelmed and overawed by
the Christianized outlook of Westerners have tried to prove that
the real aim of the Quran was to put an end to polygamy (which,
in their opinion, is intrinsically evil). Since it was widely practised
at that time, however, Islam confined itself to placing
restrictions on it. Such arguments only show the mental slavery
to which these people have succumbed. That polygamy is an evil
per se is an unacceptable proposition, for under certain
conditions it becomes a moral and social necessity. If polygamy
is totally prohibited men who cannot remain satisfied with only
one wife will look outside the bounds of matrimonial life and
create sexual anarchy and corruption. This is likely to cause
much greater harm than polygamy to the moral and social order.
For this reason the Quran has allowed those who feel the need
for it to resort to polygamy.'

Maududi, *Tafhim al-Quran*, ii, 7–8: commentary on Quran 4: 3

'It [co-wife] is a terrible word – my pen almost halts in writing
it – women's mortal enemy . . . How many hearts has it broken,
how many minds has it confused and homes destroyed, how
much evil brought and how many innocents sacrificed and
prisoners taken for whom it was the origin of personal calamity?
. . . [It is] a terrible word laden with savagery and selfishness . . .
Bear in mind that as you amuse yourself with your new bride you
cause another's despair to flow in tears . . . and children whom you
taught to sorrow, weep for her tears . . . You hear the drums and
pipes [at a wedding] and they hear only the beat of misery.'

Malak Hifni Nassef (1886–1918), quoted in Leila Ahmed, *Women and Gender
in Islam: Historical Roots of a Modern Debate* (New Haven: Yale University
Press, 1992), 182

If theory is sometimes harsher than practice in upholding marital fidelity, the converse can apply with regard to inheritance. In many Muslim lands, women have been systematically denied their inheritance rights guaranteed under Islamic law, either by family pressures or by legal devices such as the family *waqf*, or trust. Marriage between first cousins, permitted under Islamic law, is often converted into a positive injunction, with girls *obliged* to marry their first cousins. The aim of such customs has been to keep property in the patriarchal family, countering the distributive effects of the laws of inheritance which allow women to inherit a portion of their parents' wealth.

### Sukayna's example

'[Sukayna] made one of her husbands sign a marriage contract that officially specified her right to *nushuz* (contestation), that rebellion against marital control that so tormented the *fuqaha* [juris consults]. She claimed the right and paraded it, like her beauty and her talent, to assert the importance and vitality of women in the Arab tradition. Admiring and respectful, the historians delight in evoking her family dramas – for instance, the case she brought against one of her husbands who had violated the rule of monogamy that she had imposed on him in the marriage contract. Dumbfounded by the conditions in the contract, the judge nevertheless was obliged to hear the case, with his own wife attending this trial of the century and the caliph sending him an emissary to keep him au courant with the course of the trial.'

Fatima Mernissi, *Women and Islam: An Historical and Theological Enquiry*, tr. Mary Jo Lakeland (Oxford: Blackwell, 1991), 192

Marriage in Islam is contractual, and given that contracts are negotiable, reformers and modernizers have argued that legal imbalances can be countered by specific contractual provisions, for instance by following the example of the Prophet Muhammad's great-granddaughter Sukayna bint Hussein who stipulated that her husband remain monogamous. However, not all the legal schools accept the woman's right to set the terms of the contract in this way and in any case her ability to do so is likely to be contingent on the power and status of her family. Just as in modern Pakistan it is not the women from upper-class families who suffer from harassment in the market, not least because they are driven around by male chauffeurs, so aristocratic women like Sukayna were spared the insecurities and indignities experienced by lower-class women.

## Marriage and divorce

Marriage is positively enjoined in Islam, and young people are urged to marry with the explicit objective of avoiding exposure to sexual temptation. 'Young men, those of you who can support a wife should marry, for it keeps you from looking at women and preserves your chastity', says one of al-Bukhari's *hadiths*. Under the Shari'a, the marriage contract – *nikah* – is a legal contract sanctioned by the divine law. It is not, as in Christianity, a sacrament. According to most legal authorities the woman's *wali* or guardian (usually her father) enters into the marriage on her behalf and most agree that a virgin may be required to marry a man of her father's choice. Only the Shi'ia view the woman 'as a full legal entity coequal with her male counterpart'. A Muslim woman's interest is supposed to be secured by the *mahr*, or dowry, provided by her husband, a sum of money or its equivalent in household goods and chattels, which remains in her possession should her husband initiate divorce.

The husband has the right of divorce by *talaq* – repudiation or unilateral declaration. He must pronounce the formula 'I divorce you' three times; the first two declarations are followed by the so-called '*idda*, or waiting period of three menstrual cycles to ensure that the woman is free from pregnancy, or, if pregnant, to ensure the husband's paternity. During this period family and friends are encouraged to effect a reconciliation. If this fails the third declaration finalizes the divorce, without recourse to a court. A man will usually have custody of his children beyond the age of seven for boys or nine for girls. If the wife initiates divorce, a procedure known as *khul'*, she sacrifices her *mahr*, or dowry. Muslim men are permitted to marry non-Muslim women from the People of the Book – i.e. Jews and Christians. The reverse does not apply. Contemporary Muslim writers such as Dr Yusuf al-Qaradawi argue that the lack of symmetry in this respect is based on the presumption that the man is head of the household. Whereas Muslims are bound to respect the religious rights of Christian and Jewish wives, there is no guarantee that Jewish or Christian husbands will safeguard a Muslim wife's freedom of worship. Other observers, however, see the rule as an unambiguous assertion of Muslim supremacism. A Lebanese anthropologist, Fuad Khuri, notes that the same pattern, whereby the dominant caste allows its sons but not its daughters to marry outside the group, prevails among Lebanon's divided communities. Where Shi'ia predominate, Shi'i men may marry Sunni women, but not vice versa; where Sunnis are dominant, the converse applies. Similar rules and conventions used to apply to riding animals, with the dominant group allowing itself the use of horses while the subordinate group was restricted to riding mules and donkeys; to the heights of buildings where dominion was expressed architecturally, and to clothes, with the dominant groups wearing sober colours – bright colours being associated with children and lower-status groups.

## The submissive wife

'It is not lawful for a woman who believes in Allah to allow anyone in her husband's house while he dislikes it. She should not go out of the house if he dislikes it and should not obey anyone who contradicts his orders. She should not refuse to share his bed [meaning that she should not deny him sexual access when he

> desires it – Trans.]. She should not beat him (in case she is stronger than he). If he is more in the wrong than she, she should plead with him until he is reconciled. If he accepts her pleading well and good, and her plea will be accepted by Allah; while if he is not reconciled with her, her plea will have reached Allah in any case.'
>
> *Hadith* reported by al-Hakim, quoted in Qaradawi, 204.

## Temporary marriage

Patriarchal assumptions pervade the Shari'a as interpreted by most traditionalists. A man's right to sexual satisfaction is divinely mandated: a man's wife does not have the right to refuse his sexual demands. Among the Twelver Shi'a men's sexual privileges are taken a stage further by means of the temporary marriage contract (*mut'a or sigheh*), which may be signed for a fixed period of time ranging from one hour to ninety-nine years. While critics see the institution as a form of legalized prostitution, leading figures in the Islamic Republic of Iran have actively promoted it, arguing that it constitutes 'an ethically and morally superior alternative to the "free" relations between the sexes prevalent in the West'.

## Islam and sexuality

'There is no monkery in Islam', runs a well-known *hadith*. 'Copulate and procreate', runs another 'for I shall gain glory from your numbers at the Day of Judgement.' The Prophet of Islam is celebrated as enjoying not just the company of women but the pleasures of sex. After Khadija's death, he is said to have married at least nine women, possibly as many as thirteen. *Hadiths* proclaim his virility: one in al-Bukhari's collection claims he had intercourse with nine of his wives in a single night. Christian polemicists used such images to depict the Prophet as a monster of sensuality. Modern Muslim apologists have reacted defensively, insisting that Muhammad's marriages were either political – aimed at cementing tribal alliances – or designed to provide social security for the women, several of whom were widows. While both these explanations are convincing in the context of a pastoral nomadic society where polygyny was the norm they need not exclude the image of Muhammad as the ideal typical charismatic leader, a figure classically associated with sexual prowess. (Another example is the polygamous Mormon Prophet Joseph Smith.) However, the presence of such stories in the literature probably tells us as much about the expectations surrounding leadership as anything that can be factually determined about Muhammad's personal predilections. His sexuality, like that of Christ, opens up a range of interpretative possibilities. Setting aside the historical question, his multiple marriages testify to a positive attitude towards human sexuality which contrasts strikingly with the asceticism of the early Christian Church. At the core of its vision, according to the Tunisian scholar Abdelwahab Bouhdiba, Islam reflects a 'lyrical view of life'. The pleasures of sex are a foretaste of paradise as described in the Quran and elaborated by the exegetes into the 'infinite orgasm' – the state of ecstasy that ultimately leads to the beatific vision and union with God. In the post-Freudian age language and images that appalled and disgusted Christians of a more prudish era deserve to be appreciated for the life-affirming message they impart.

## A foretaste of paradise

'Sexual desire as a manifestation of God's wisdom has, independently of its manifest function, another function: when the individual yields to it and satisfies it, he experiences a delight which would be without match if it were lasting. It is a foretaste of the delights secured for men in Paradise, because to make a promise to men of delights they have not tasted would be ineffective . . . This earthly delight, imperfect because limited in time, is a powerful motivation to incite men to try and attain the perfect delight, the eternal delight, and therefore urges men to

## Women in social and religious life

In the classical traditions, the positive value of sexuality is affirmed, but it is also perceived as dangerous and potentially destructive of the social order determined by God. The bias against celibacy prevents the emergence of a distinctive caste of the female religious comparable to the nuns and abbesses of the Christian West. The sense that good social order is contingent on regulating sexuality – particularly female sexuality – becomes institutionalized. The seclusion of women is justified by fear of female sexual power: an atavistic cultural memory, perhaps, of the female deities destroyed by the prophet of the triumphant singular God.

Gender differences are strongly emphasized, God having created humans male and female, and any aspect of behaviour in dress or comportment that clouds the distinction is discouraged or forbidden. Homosexuality, in this view, is a major sin, 'a reversal of the natural order, a corruption of man's sexuality and a crime against the rights of females'. Men should grow beards in order to distinguish themselves from infidels. 'Be different from the polytheists,' says a *hadith* in al-Bukhari's collection: 'let the beard grow and trim the mustache.' It is *makruh* (disapproved of) to shave the beard or drastically to cut or shorten it, but it is *mustahabb* (commendable) 'to remove something from its length and breadth if it grows big'.

According to traditional interpretations of the law, a married woman's social circle – apart from her husband – must be confined to female friends and her *mahrams* – which includes those male members of her extended family whom she cannot marry by law. These are fathers, sons, brothers, foster-brothers, nephews, and male in-laws. Although local customs vary, the taboo on female association with men outside the *mahram* relationship is widespread in Muslim societies from Morocco to South Asia. These patterns, however, are not universal. In parts of Africa south of the Sahara, Islamic law has become mixed with local traditions giving women substantially greater rights in marriage and divorce. Among some Muslim communities in South-East Asia, there are no traditions of seclusion and elements of matrilineal customs survive even among the pious. Here, the Shari'a is seen in terms of religious and ethical duties (*'ibadat*) rather than social practices (*mu'amalat*), where local customary law has priority.

In the Middle East and South Asia and other parts of the Muslim world, the extended kinship group sustained by the *mahram* taboo was basic to the social structure. The contrast with the development of Western societies is striking. In the medieval West, the Church sustained deliberate policies against kin-based groups, encouraging distance-marriages, insisting that the Church as the corporate body of Christ transcend and supersede the biological ties of kinship. As the Church was gradually replaced by civil bodies, from cities to trading corporations, class interests and divisions emerged which in due course became the locus of social conflicts and hence the subject of historical change. Women's emancipation was predicated on the emancipation of *men* from the bonds of kinship, with profession, trade, or class eventually acting as co-determinants of an individual's identity along with 'family background'. There being no church in Islam to compete with the family as focus of allegiance, the individual remained much more closely tied to the bonds of kinship. Women may sometimes have enjoyed an honoured and protected position in this system, but their freedom was limited in proportion to their reproductive capacity as genetic carriers and bearers of kinship identity. Today, the legacy of the privileged status the family had under the Shariʿa continues to militate against the assertion of alternative institutions or solidarities based on free association or common purpose. In many Muslim countries, public institutions have been subverted or undermined by the persistence of kinship solidarities: examples include the bitterly contested Baʿth (Renaissance) party in Syria, dominated for decades by a network of families belonging to the minority Shiʿa ʿAlawi sect who ruled over a Sunni majority, and Iraq where a Sunni minority from the Tikrit area ruled over Shiʿi majority until removed by the US-led invasion of 2003.

8. Detail of *mashrabiya*, Cairo. These wooden lattice overhangs, a familiar feature of pre-modern domestic architecture in the Middle East, enhanced ventilation while ensuring female privacy

The exclusion of women from the public domain in the main Islamic centres inevitably led to their exclusion from the religious domain as well. In Cairo, for example – as described by Edward Lane in the 1820s – women were forbidden to pray alongside men in the mosques because 'the Muslims are of the opinion that the presence of females inspires a very different kind of devotion from that which is requisite in a place dedicated to the worship of God'. Female exclusion was reinforced by pollution taboos over menstruation, childbirth, and contact with young children. The *hadith* collections contain detailed sections on ritual impurities, and it is generally women who are disadvantaged by the rules. Women participate in some Sufi practices and are often associated with visits to the tombs of saints or 'friends' of God – activities often disapproved of by the *'ulama*. In the more tradition-bound sections of society, female religiosity is more likely to find expression in activities disapproved of by the pious, such as the *zar* or spirit possession cults still widespread in Egypt and North Africa. In some instances, these spirits are said to be forcing their 'hosts' to resist the veil: *baladi* (country) women ordered to cover themselves in accordance with Islamist demands are 'possessed' by spirits which cause them to fall sick if they do so.

## Women, colonialism, and the family

The collapse of the majority of the world's Muslim states before European military power during the colonial era made the family the primary refuge of Muslim identity. 'Men often ridiculed and rejected in the new colonial governmental and economic structures, found their families a sanctuary, a representation of Islamic religious values wherein they were honoured.' If the family was a sacred area, relatively free from the humiliations imposed by colonial overlords, the woman was its centre, 'the hub around which all its economic, personal and political activities revolved'. Family law was the core of the Shari'a: because of its sacred resonances, reforming governments were reluctant to tamper with it, despite changes introduced in the areas of civil, commercial, and penal law. When reforms were introduced they were perceived by traditionalists as coming from a hostile West. Wealthy women such as Hoda Sharawi in Egypt were the first to throw off the veil, a symbol of oppression for emancipated upper-class women, but for others it developed into a symbol of cultural authenticity.

### Family values

'The Muslim family is the miniature of the whole of Muslim society and its firm basis. In it the man or father functions as the imam in accordance with the patriarchal nature of Islam. The religious responsibility of the family rests upon his shoulders...In the family the father upholds the tenets of the religion and his authority symbolizes that of God in the world. The man is in fact respected in the family precisely because of the sacerdotal function that he fulfils. The rebellion of Muslim women in certain quarters of Islamic society came when men themselves ceased to fulfil their religious function and lost their virile and patriarchal character. By becoming themselves effeminate they caused the ensuing reaction of revolt among certain women who no longer felt the authority of religion upon themselves.'

Seyyed Hossein Nasr, *Ideals and Realities of Islam* (London: Allen & Unwin, 1966; repr. 1975), 110

## Sartorial politics

Costume and physical appearance in pre-modern societies was never a matter of purely personal choice. In the West until quite recently, dress was the primary external indicator of status, class, and trade. Dress codes still play an important part in many educational institutions and uniforms are an essential component of the corporate identities many firms still impose on their employees. In Muslim societies, where specialist crafts and skills were often the preserve of particular ethnic groups, dress and physical appearance went together. Members of ethnic minorities such as the Lurs of western Iran who specialized as porters in Baghdad, could be identified by a particular type of felt hat worn by men. The different Sufi orders were characterized by the style of their turbans and the folds of their gowns. Reforming autocrats in the 19th and 20th centuries often attempted to eliminate local allegiances by insisting on standardized headgear. The best-known example was the Ottoman Fez (a red brimless felt hat worn by men) – introduced in the 1820s in the teeth of religious opposition, only to become identified in the course of a century, with 'Islamic' rectitude. Where men were ordered to change their dress to conform to ideas of progress held by Muslim rulers, upper-class Muslim women tended to adopt European dress voluntarily, by imitating the fashions imported from Europe. The exception was in Iran, where Reza Shah Pahlavi, an illiterate Cossack sergeant who rose to become the country's ruler in the 1920s, actually ordered his female subjects to remove their *chadors* (veils).

### The virtuous woman

'The morals and manners of the Muslim woman are quite different from those of non-Muslim women and the women of the time of the *jahiliya*. The Muslim woman is chaste, dignified, self-respecting and modest, while the woman who is ignorant of the divine guidance may be vain, showy, and anxious to display her attractions. Such display includes exposing the attractive parts of the body, walking and talking in a seductive manner, displaying her ornaments, wearing revealing and sexy clothes, and the like.'

Qaradawi, 163

The standardized 'Islamic' dress worn by women in an increasing number of Muslim cities has no particular historical precedents, although it conforms in a general way to ideas of female modesty extrapolated from the Quran. Known as the *ziy shari'* and the *hijab* (veil), these tent shaped robes with nun-like wimples covering the head are designed to conceal both hair and feminine curves and are claimed by their wearers to be similar to the costumes worn by Muhammad's wives (who are ordered to protect themselves from 'behind the veil or curtain' in the only Quranic reference to female seclusion). This invented Muslim tradition first made its appearance among the female affiliates of the Muslim Brotherhood (the Muslim Sisters) during the 1930s. It became increasingly popular during the 1970s and 1980s, and generally signals support among the women wearing it for the aims of the Islamist movements. Several analysts insist adoption of the *hijab*, far from signalling the internalization by women of patriarchal attitudes, may actually represent the contrary, facilitating a new social and spatial mobility, allowing women to 'invade' public spaces previously reserved for men. By adopting 'Islamic dress' – it is argued – a woman may even defy patriarchal authority while making it plain to the non-*mahram* males she encounters of necessity outside the home that she is not sexually available, and that harassing her is tantamount to a sacrilegious act. The authority to which she considers herself answerable is no longer that of her father or brother, but that of God or perhaps the religious leader who claims to speak on his behalf. This view, however, is far from being universally accepted, and there are studies which show that the women who adopt the *hijab* are less likely than unveiled women to seek work outside the home or to be involved in higher education. In principle there is a world of difference between the situation facing women who adopt the 'veil' voluntarily and those who do so as a result of legislation or social pressures. The former are exercising freedom of choice, the latter are having their freedom to choose taken away. In reality the situation is a good deal more complex than suggested by either of these alternatives. In both Muslim majority and countries where Muslims are minorities the veil has become a symbolic marker of cultural identity, a shibboleth by which the Muslim woman is seen to proclaim her religious and political allegiance. In countries, including the Western diaspora, where other choices are possible, such an act can be a gesture of independence signalling a rejection of the prevailing, non-Muslim social mores. At Grenoble in France, a secondary school pupil who refused to remove her head-covering even for physical education classes became at once a national heroine and national pariah: 'France is my freedom, so is my veil!' she proclaimed. Often as not, however, such choices will involve a degree of pressure, from families, husbands, or peers. The semiotics of veiling vary from region to region, city to city, *dar al-islam* to *dar al-harb*. There are no generalizations that can safely be applied 'across the board'.

### Avoiding the infidel

'The Quran, the Sunna and the consensus of Muslim scholars all teach Muslims to be distinct from non-believers and in general to avoid resembling them. Anything which is likely to cause corruption in a hidden and diffuse manner is related to this matter and is likewise prohibited. The imitation of the appearance of the non-believers will lead to imitation of their immoral behaviour and evil qualities – indeed, even of their beliefs. Such influences can neither be brought under control nor easily detected, and consequently it becomes difficult or even impossible to eradicate them.'

*Kitab Iqtida al-Sirat al-Mustaqim*, cited in Qadarawi, 95

9. The tent-like *burqa*, completely covering her body, through which an Afghan woman surveys the world. Displacement following on decades of war has increased pressures for female segregation and seclusion

## Legal reforms and the backlash against them

In recent decades, under pressure from reformers, attempts have been made to rectify some of the legal inequalities facing women – for example, by restricting the right of unilateral divorce, or requiring that a wife register her permission with the court before her husband avails himself of the right to additional wives. Several countries have raised the minimum age of marriage. Nowadays it generally stands at 18 for boys, varying from 15 to 18 for girls, depending on the country. After the Iranian Revolution of 1979, however, the victorious clergy abolished the Family Protection Law introduced by the Shah, which set the age of marriage at 18 for girls and boys, restoring the minimum to 15 for boys and 9 for girls (though after strong female protests, this was raised to 13).

Lowering the age of marriage is evidently designed to strengthen the patriarchal family against the pressures of individualism since parents are able to exercise more influence on younger people, especially girls, in their choice of marriage partners. At the same time established social networks are breaking down under the pressures of rapid urbanization and economic change: everywhere women are exposed to encounters with men outside their *mahram* groups, encounters still deemed by many to be fraught with sexual danger. Governments, such as that of Pakistan, have responded to populist demands for a 'return' to the Shari'a by enacting laws which introduce Shari'a penalties. In 1979 the military government of General Zia ul Haqq introduced the Hudood Ordinance prescribing the Quranic punishments for *zina*, theft, drinking, and false accusations of *zina*. By insisting on Quranic standards of proof the Ordinance makes it difficult for a woman to bring charges of rape without risking a counter-accusation of *zina*, with the rules of evidence weighted against her.

# Islam and feminism

Muslim feminists argue that it is not Islam as such, but rather reactionary male interpretations of the faith that are invoked to justify patriarchal attitudes. As suggested earlier the logic of this position inevitably comes up against certain discriminatory provisions in the divine text of the Quran. A modernist hermeneutic stating that the Quranic provisions are time-contingent rather than absolute becomes necessary before the contradiction between the spiritual and moral equality of women and their legal inequality can be resolved. The argument that a woman giving evidence on a business matter might need assistance from her friend might make sense under pre-modern conditions when most women were illiterate, but as the Quranic rules stand, the testimony of a woman with an MBA is only worth half that of an illiterate male. Beyond such textual sticking points, however, there are areas where masculine or androcentric interpretations are being contested, particularly in the field of hadith, where the questioning of sources belongs to a time-honoured methodology and is less controversial than taking issue with the text of the Quran. The biggest obstacles facing Muslim feminists are cultural and historical: feminism is perceived as coming from a hostile source.

One strategy for defusing the accusation that the Muslim feminist critic of Islamic attitudes is simply a Western-inspired lackey is the 'indigenous feminist' approach adopted by several women writers, notably the Moroccan Fatima Mernissi and the Egyptian-born Leila Ahmed. Both writers see a contradiction between the ethical principles of Islam with its commitment to social justice regardless of gender and the restrictions to which Muslim women became increasingly subjugated. For Ahmed the practices sanctioned by Muhammad in the first Muslim society reflect far more positive attitudes than became current during the later 'Abbasid era, when concubinage, sanctioned if not encouraged by Islam, became widespread. She believes that if the ethical voice of Islam had been attended to, it would have significantly tempered the 'extreme androcentric bias' of the law. Access to slaves and concubines led to women being treated as commodities, as upper-class women became increasingly marginalized. Mernissi, adopting a similar line of argument, claims that the women of the Prophet's day were relatively free. They participated with men in the public domain, if not in battle, and were active in the early Islamic movement. According to the majority of traditions, Khadija, Muhammad's trusted wife, was the 'first Muslim', the first in Muhammad's household to accept that Muhammad's messages came from God. After her death Muhammad married many women, some of them for political reasons, others apparently for love. His favourite wife 'Aisha, daughter of his close companion Abu Bakr became the source of numerous *hadiths*. She was a major political actor in the civil war or strife (*fitna*) following the assassination of the third caliph 'Uthman in 656. Her role as a source of *hadiths* is so important that in one tradition the Prophet is supposed to have told the Muslims that they 'received half their religion from a woman'. Mernissi documents personal tensions between 'Aisha and Abu Huraira, a Companion of the Prophet who heads a great many chains of hadith transmitters, seeing in him the source of numerous anti-feminist *hadiths* that eventually gained currency. Mernissi's method, as Andrew Rippin points out, shares with that of the Islamists a tendency towards the remythologization of society, with both sides selectively citing the evidence to suit their arguments.

## Two voices

'There appear...to be two distinct voices within Islam, and two competing understandings of gender, one expressed in the pragmatic regulations for society...the other in the articulation of an ethical vision. Even as Islam instituted marriage as a sexual hierarchy in its ethical voice – a voice virtually unheard by rulers and lawmakers – it insistently stressed the importance of the spiritual and ethical dimensions of being and the equality of all individuals. While the first voice has been extensively elaborated into a body of political and legal thought, which constitutes the technical understanding of Islam, the second – the voice to which ordinary believing Muslims, who are essentially ignorant of the details of Islam's technical legacy, give their assent – has left little trace on the political and legal heritage of Islam. The unmistakable presence of ethical egalitarianism explains why Muslim women frequently insist, often inexplicably to non-Muslims, that Islam is not sexist. They hear and read in its sacred text, justly and legitimately, a different message from that heard by the makers and enforcers of orthodox, androcentric Islam.'

Ahmed, Women and Gender in Islam, 65–6

## Conclusion

The symbolism conveyed by veiling may be ambiguous, but there can be no doubt that Muslim women are becoming a force to be reckoned with in the public domain. Even Saudi Arabia, bastion of Islamic sexual apartheid, has witnessed public demonstrations by women protesting against corruption and rulings forbidding them to drive motor vehicles. Among the less affluent, labour migration forces changes in the sexual division of labour, with a significant proportion of households now headed by women. Universities in both Muslim majority countries and the industrialized North, are producing more and more Muslim female graduates. In Iran, for example, despite the formal reintroduction of child marriage, the mean age of first marriages for young women has continued to rise from around 19 before the revolution to 24 today – with nearly 80% married after the age of 20. With young women from rural families seeing education as the path to economic independence, a majority of college students are now women. 'Companionate marriage', with couples freely choosing their partners, is becoming the norm. Women – wearing headscarves, or bare-headed – were prominent in the 'Arab Spring' that brought down the regimes in Tunisia and Egypt in 2011. In the United States, where the *hijab* became *de rigueur* for activist Muslim women in the polarized atmosphere following 9/11, when it seemed important for them to asserts their rights as Muslims *and* Americans, a movement towards 'de-jabbing' – abandoning the headscarf – is gaining momentum. Sartorial coding – expressing one's identity or affiliation by means of dress – is a characteristic of all modern societies, and modernity is universal. Despite its reactionary rhetoric, the Islamic revolution is being remorselessly carried on its tide.

# Chapter 6
# **The two _jihads_**

## Introduction

_Jihad_, like the word _fatwa_, is an Islamic term that has entered the contemporary lexicon, not least because of its use by modern Islamist movements such as al-Qaeda that have been actively involved in terrorism, kidnapping and other violent activities. In its primary meaning the word means 'exertion' or 'struggle', and its use in the traditional Islamic discourse is very far from being confined to military matters. The usual translation 'holy war' is therefore misleading. Many forms of activity are included under the term. In the classical formulations the believer may undertake _jihad_ 'by his heart; his tongue; his hands; and by the sword' – the foremost of these being the first.

_Jihad_ is collective obligation for Muslims – a duty known as _fard kifaya_, distinct from the purely personal obligations of prayer, fasting, and pilgrimage. It can be undertaken by the ruler on behalf of the whole community – and thus becomes, in the course of time, an instrument of policy. The classical doctrine of _jihad_ was formulated during the centuries of conquest, when the faith sustained an outward momentum unprecedented in human history. The doctrine was both an expression of Islamic triumphalism and an attempt, comparable to the concept of the just war in Roman law, to limit the consequences of war. Adapting the customs of pre-Islamic bedouin warfare, an element of chivalry was built into the code: women and children, the old and the sick, were to be spared. Polytheists were faced with the choice of conversion or death, but the Peoples of the Book – initially Jews and Christians, later extended to Zoroastrians, Hindus, and others – were to be protected in return for payment of taxes (the *jizya*, a poll tax, and the *kharaj*, a tax on land). In some commentaries, the *dhimmis* (as the protected minorities are called) are to be deliberately humiliated when paying the tax. Though justified by the argument that the *dhimmis* are exempt from military duties and from the payment of *zakat*, the *jizya* is also, like the rules of marriage, an example of Islamic supremacism. This is not religious tolerance in accordance with the values of post-Enlightenment liberalism. But it falls short of the position necessary to sustain the charge that Islam 'converts by the sword'. Polytheists get short shrift, and there is no question that in parts of Africa and Asia today people adhering to animist cults have been subject to forcible Islamization. By the standards of medieval Europe, however, the doctrine of *jihad* is a good deal more humane than papal bulls urging the extirpation of heretics. The People of the Book who accept Islamic rule are allowed to practise their religion freely, and, since Islam defines religion in broadly orthopraxist terms – emphasizing rules of behaviour over issues of belief – this meant in practice that religious minorities enjoyed a limited form of self-government. The Islamic record of tolerance in pre-modern times compares very favourably with that of the medieval Church.

Nevertheless, the classical doctrine, as interpreted politically, does imply that Islam will ultimately prove victorious. Following the logic of *jihad* the world is divided into two mutually hostile camps: the sphere of Islam (*dar al-islam*) and the sphere of War (*dar al-harb*). Enemies will convert, like the polytheists, or submit, like the Christians and Jews. Those who die in 'the path of God' are instantly translated to paradise, without waiting for the resurrection or judgement day. They are buried where they fall, their bodies spared the ritual of cleansing in a mosque. The martyrs are pure already.

Just as the first Christians were obliged to postpone, indefinitely, the second coming of Christ, so the global triumph of Islam had to be deferred. The outward momentum of conquest was checked – before Constantinople, at Poitiers, and in India. The divinely appointed universal order came up against intransigent realities, such as geographical barriers, or revitalized Hindu or Christian states. Formerly Muslim territories such as Sicily and Spain reverted to unbelief. In due course the concept of *dar al-islam* was modified. As the divine law was communal, rather than territorial, in its application, the scholars disputed amongst themselves about the number of Muslims required to make a territory *dar al-islam*. Must the Muslims have political control, or was it merely a matter of their right to proclaim the message of Islam and to perform their religious duties? As with so many questions of law, there were no conclusive answers. The jurists disagreed about whether a particular territory was *dar al-islam* or *dar al-harb* – or in a state of suspended warfare indicated by such intermediate categories such as *dar al-sulh* (Sphere of Truce).

## The greater *jihad*

According to a well-known hadith, the Prophet distinguished between the 'lesser' *jihad* of war against the polytheists and the 'greater' jihad against evil. At its broadest, the latter was the struggle in which the virtuous Muslim was engaged throughout his or her life. Despite the *élan* of the early conquests, historically it was the 'greater' *jihad* which sustained the expansion of Islam in many parts of the world. The dualism of good versus evil, *dar al-islam* against *dar al-harb*, was maintained less by territorial concepts than by legal observance. *Dar al-islam* was where the law prevailed. In pre-colonial times, before the military might of the West erupted into Muslim consciousness, that law was commensurate with civilization itself. The high culture of Cairo and Baghdad extended via the trade routes to southern Africa, northern India, and south-east Asia.

The process of expansion was organic and self-directing. Since there was no church or overarching religious institution, there was no universal, centrally directed missionary effort. There was, however, the demonstration effect of Muslims living literate, orderly, and sober lives. The travels of Ibn Battuta attest to the exuberant variety of a world bound together by a common faith in God and his Prophet and a common holy book and, to a lesser degree, by common practices, as well as to the prestige of its high culture. When the famous traveller from Tangier found himself in the Maldive islands, he was automatically expected to undertake the office of *qadi* because of his knowledge of the law.

**10. The Great Mosque of Niono, Mali. Patterns of mosque design proliferated as Islam spread into different cultural regions, absorbing local vernaculars and providing opportunities for collective artistic achievements of the highest order**

## The Sufi *tariqas*

This self-same process of organic expansion along the trade routes, or among semi-settled pastoralists, was sustained by the Sufi *tariqas*, the 'mystical orders' of Islam. As we saw in Chapter 3, the Sufi adepts were engaged in ascetic and mystical practices aimed at releasing their minds from worldly attachments and eventually achieving the state of union or 'abiding' with God. The same religious impulses are found in many places, from India to western Asia and North Africa. In Christianity they find expression among individual pietists as well as in the vast and variegated traditions of monasticism. In Islam mystical practices follow the same developmental logic as oral scriptures. Just as every hadith is supplied with a line of transmitters (*isnad*) tracing it back to the Prophet, so the different Sufi disciplines or rules (Arab. *tariqa*, literally 'path') are provided with a chain (*silsila*) of authorities extending back to the Prophet, his earliest Companions, and the eponymous founders of the various orders. From the mid-12th century until modern times, the Sufi brotherhoods flourished all over the Islamic world, from rural outbacks to the dense human fabric of the cities. It would be wrong to see the Sufis as necessarily 'withdrawn' from the world. Although some of the Sufi brotherhoods indulged in ritual practices regarded with hostility by the *'ulama*, the majority insisted that inner reality of Islam (*haqiqa*) could only be approached through observance of Shari'a, the outward or exoteric law. Under the umbrella of their different *tariqas* the brotherhoods developed formidable organizations bound by personal ties of allegiance to their leaders. The common spiritual disciplines of the orders, the gradations of spiritual authority linking the leader with his followers, the leader's intercessionary powers with God and duty of obedience owed to him: all of these made the *tariqas* important sources of social and hence political power – especially in peripheral areas such as the central Asian steppes, the Sahel, and tropical parts of Africa. Even at the centres of empire the orders were sometimes seen as a threat: for example by the Ottoman Sultan Mahmud II, who suppressed the Bektashi order in 1826.

11. The Islamic Society of America's mosque near Indianapolis, Indiana. There may be as many as eight million Muslims in the United States. If numbers continue to grow at the current rate Islam may soon displace Judaism as the country's largest non-Christian religion

## The traveller

Muhammad ibn 'Abdulla ibn Battuta (1304–77) travelled for quarter of a century after making the pilgrimage to Makka, visiting Anatolia, Constantinople, Persia, the Crimea, India, and China. In the Maldive islands he reluctantly accepted the post of judge or *Qadi*. The following is an extract from his account:

'The people of the Maldive Islands are upright and pious, sound in belief and sincere in thought; their bodies are weak, they are unused to fighting, and their armour is prayer. Once when I ordered a thief's hand to be cut off, a number of those in the room fainted. The Indian pirates do not raid or molest them, as they have learned from experience that anyone who seizes anything from them speedily meets misfortune. In each island of theirs there are beautiful mosques and most of their buildings are made of wood...Their womenfolk do not cover their hands, not even their queen does so, and they comb their hair and gather it to one side. Most of them wear only an apron from their waists to the ground, the rest of their bodies being uncovered. While I held the qadiship there I tried to put an end to this practice and ordered them to wear clothes, but I met with no success. No woman was admitted my presence in a lawsuit unless her body was covered, but apart from that I was unable to effect anything.'

From *Ibn Battuta Travels in Asia and Africa: 1325–1354*, tr. H. A. R. Gibb (New York, 1929), 241 ff

12. Dancing Sufis from a 17th-century Turkish book. The 'Whirling Dervishes' hope to achieve a state of ecstasy or higher spiritual consciousness by ritualized spinning to music

## *Jihad* and resistance

The strife against evil, the 'greater *jihad*', might take a purely moralistic form; but at times of increasingly traumatic historical crisis, the 'lesser *jihad*' came to the fore. The two jihads were interchangeable. The most active movements of resistance to European rule during the 19th and early 20th centuries were led or inspired by renovators (*mujaddids*), most of them members of Sufi orders, who sought to emulate the Prophet's example by purifying the religion of their day and waging war on corruption and infidelity. Such movements included the rebellion led by Prince Dipanegara in Java (1825–30), the *jihad* preached among the Yusufzai Pathans on the Northwest Frontier of India by Sayyid Ahmad Barelwi in 1831, the Naqshabandi Chechen leader Shamil's campaign against the Russians in the Caucasus (1834–59), and 'Abd al-Qadir's *jihad* against the French in Algeria (1839–47). Not all of these movements were directed at resisting Europeans: the Mahdi Muhammad ibn 'Abdullah in the Sudan originally campaigned against the imperial ambitions of the Egyptians or 'Turks' he believed had abandoned Islam to foreigners; the 'New Sect' in China, led by another Naqshbandi sheikh Ma Ming Hsin, was behind a series of major revolts against the Sinicizing policies of the Manchu emperors during the 19th century.

## Reformists and modernists

Once it became clear that Muslim arms were no match for the overwhelming technical and military superiority of the Europeans or nominally Muslim governments backed by them, the movement for Islamic renewal took an intellectually radical turn. Among the élites which had been exposed most directly to the European presence, the catastrophic failure of Islam was seen to lie as much in education and culture as in military defeat. A return to the pristine forms of Islam would not be enough to guarantee the survival of Islam as a civilization and way of life. The more sophisticated renovators may be divided very broadly into reformists and modernists. Reformists usually came from the ranks of the 'ulama and were more concerned with religious renewal from within the tradition. One of their most influential reformist centres was the college of Deoband in northern India, founded in 1867. The Deobandis not only attacked the cult of saints or 'friends', widespread in India, with much overlapping between Islamic and Hindu styles of devotion. They adopted a modernist stance in emphasizing personal responsibility in observance of the Shari'a. They made full use of modern techniques of communication, including the printing press, the postal service and the expanding railway network. Deoband contributed significantly to the emergence of India's Muslims as a self-conscious community. Unlike the modernists, however, the Deobandis tried to have as little as possible to do with the British or their government. 'To like and appreciate the customs of the infidels', wrote a leading Deobandi 'alim, Mawlana Ashraf 'Ali Thanawi, 'is a grave sin.' In the rural areas which were harder for them to reach their work would eventually be complemented by the Tablighi Jama'at founded by a graduate of Deoband, Maulana Muhammad Ilyas (1885–1944).

Modernism was the doctrine of the political élites and intelligentsias which had most exposure to European culture. They recognized that in order to regain political power Muslims would have to adopt European military techniques, modernize their economies and administrations, and introduce modern forms of education. On the religious front, they argued for a new hermeneutic or reinterpretation of the faith in the light of modern conditions. The modernists' fascination with Europe and its works often led them to adopt Western clothes and Western lifestyles which in due course separated them from the more traditionally minded classes. It was from modernist circles that veil-ripping feminists and the leaders of nationalist movements tended to be drawn.

There are no clear lines dividing the two tendencies, which merge and divide according to circumstance. Leaders of both currents such as Sir Sayyid Ahmad Khan, founder of the Anglo-Oriental College (later University) of Aligarh in India, and reformers like Muhammad 'Abduh (d. 1906) founder of the Salafiya movement in Egypt, tended to reside in the cultural centres of the Muslim world that had been most exposed to Western influences. Their problem was not, as 'Abduh's patron Lord Cromer (virtual ruler of Egypt between 1883 and 1907) would argue, that Islam was beyond reform; but rather that there was no institutional hierarchy comparable to that of the Christian churches through which theological and legal reforms could be effected. Reformist *'ulama* like 'Abduh or his more conservative disciple Rashid Rida had no special authority through which they could impose their views and many of their peers among the *'ulama* remained unreconstructed traditionalists up till the present.

## Sayyid Ahmed Khan

The most influential modernist thinker to appear in 19th-century India was Sir Sayyid Ahmed Khan (1817–98), founder of the Muhammadan Anglo-Oriental College at Aligarh where modern arts and sciences were taught, in English, alongside traditional Islamic studies. A former employee of the East India Company, his aim was to produce an elite of educated Muslims able to compete with Hindus for jobs in the Indian administration. Survival lay in modernizing Islamic thought and institutions. Exercising personal *ijtihad* based on a study of the Quran's Arabic idiom, Sayyid Ahmed Khan made a fundamental distinction between the details of revelation (*furu'*) which, he argued, referred to specific historical circumstances, and the general principles (*usul*) underlying them. In principle, he believed that the laws of God as revealed through the Shari'a were identical with the laws of nature, since the Final Cause or Creator God ultimately determined the causal relationships governing all material and non-material things.

## Reinterpreting theology

The following is an extract from a document, the Fifteen Principles, Sir Sayyid submitted to the 'Ulama of Saharanpur in 1873 or 1874:

- Whichever verses of the Glorious Quran may seem to us to contradict truth or reality, there are two explanations of such a seeming contradiction: either we have made an error in understanding the meaning of these verses, or we are mistaken in our understanding of what is truth and reality. No word of any traditionist or exegete can be regarded as authentic in opposition to it – i.e. to the word of the Glorious Quran.
- In religious matters we are bound to obey the *sunna* of the Prophet and Islam, in worldly matters we are allowed to do so [but it is not binding on us]. By the word *sunna* I mean the precepts of religion, that is all.
- As to the explicitly revealed precepts in matters of religion (*din*), the binding character of such precepts is certain. But the remaining questions which are open to the exercise of independent judgment (*ijtihad* and analogical reasoning *qiyas*) are all conjectural.
- All the precepts of the religion of Islam are in conformity with nature. Were not this so, one would have to hold a blind person guilty for not seeing and a person with eyesight guilty for seeing.
- Actions that have been commanded are good in themselves and actions that have been forbidden are bad in themselves. The Prophet only informs us about their good or bad quality like a doctor who informs about the harm and benefit of [different] medicines.

From Christian W. Troll, *Sayyid Ahmad Khan: A Reinterpretation of Muslim Theology* (New Delhi: Vikas Publishing House, 1978)

## The end of the caliphate

On 11 November 1914, the Ottoman Sultan and Caliph Mehmet V declared a jihad or holy war against Russia, France, and Great Britain, announcing that it had become an obligation for all Muslims, whether young or old, on foot or mounted, to support the struggle with their goods and money. The proclamation, which took the form of a *fatwa*, was endorsed by religious leaders throughout the Sultan's dominions. Outside the Empire, however, its effect was minimal. In Russian central Asia, French North Africa and British India the colonial authorities generally had no difficulty in finding *'ulama* to publicly endorse the Allied cause. Most galling for the Sultan-Caliph, his suzerain the Sharif Hussein of Makka, Guardian of the Holy Places, refused to endorse the jihad publicly. He had already been approached by the British with a view to launching an Arab revolt against the Turks – the revolt whose success would eventually result in the Sharif's sons Faisal and 'Abdullah being given the British-protected thrones of Iraq and Jordan. The Arabs of Syria, Mesopotamia, Palestine, and the Hejaz preferred freedom to 'Islamic' rule, even though for many that freedom entailed the risk (soon to be realized) of a new colonialist domination under the 'infidel'. Then, as now, pan-Islamic solidarity proved an illusion.

The collapse of the Ottoman armies in 1917–18 drove the point home. A revitalized Turkish nation under Mustafa Kemal took the ultimate step of abolishing the caliphate in 1924, bringing the crisis of Islamic legitimacy to a head. Though the decision was endorsed by the Turkish National Assembly, and generally approved by Arab nations newly freed from Ottoman dominion, the move was preceded by a mass agitation by the Muslims of India protesting against the dismemberment of the Ottoman Empire and the removal of the final link between an existing Islamic state and the divine polity founded by the Prophet Muhammad.

# The quest for an Islamic state

The Khilafat Movement (as it is known) dramatized the fundamental contradiction between pan-Islamic and nationalist aspirations. In India, it represented a turning point in the anti-colonialist movement, as Muslims formerly appeased by Britain's Eastern Policy favouring the Ottoman interest joined Hindu nationalists in opposition to the Raj. That coalition proved short-lived, and the momentum generated by the Khilafat Movement would eventually lead to a separate political destiny for India's Muslims in the form of Pakistan.

The movement, however, evoked no response in the Arab world or not in Turkey, where the caliphate was associated with a discredited political system. For Arab nationalists, the caliphate had come to be associated with hated Ottoman rule. The Egyptian *'alim* and judge, 'Ali 'Abd al-Raziq, in a highly controversial essay published in 1925, argued that the institution had no real basis in Islam. The fact that the Prophet had combined spiritual and political roles was purely coincidental; the later caliphate did not represent a true consensus of the Muslims because it was based on force. The more conservative Rashid Rida, though once a supporter of the Ottoman caliphate, accepted its demise as symptomatic of Muslim decline; and while no advocate of secularism, he saw in the Turkish National Assembly's decision a genuine expression of the Islamic principle of consultation (*shura*). The ideal caliph, according to Rida, was an independent interpreter of the Law (*mujtahid*) who would work in concert with the *'ulama*. In the absence of a suitable candidate, and of *'ulama* versed in the modern sciences, the best alternative was for an Islamic state ruled by an enlighted élite in consultation with the people, able to interpret the Shari'a and legislate when necessary.

# The Muslim Brotherhood

Many of Rida's ideas were taken up by the most influential Sunni reform movement, the Muslim Brotherhood, founded in 1928 by

Hasan al-Banna, an Egyptian schoolteacher. The Brotherhood's original aims were moral as much as political: it sought to reform society by encouraging Islamic observance and opposing Western cultural influences, rather than by attempting to capture the state by direct political action. However, in the mounting crisis over Palestine during and after the Second World War, the Brotherhood became increasingly radicalized. In 1948, the Prime Minister Nuqrashi Pasha was assassinated by a Brotherhood member and Hasan al-Banna paid with his life in a retaliatory killing by the security services the following year.

The Brotherhood played a leading part in the disturbances that led to the overthrow of the monarchy in 1952, but after the revolution it came into conflict with the nationalist government of Gamal 'Abdul Nasser. In 1954, after an attempt on Nasser's life, the Brotherhood was again suppressed, its members imprisoned, exiled, or driven underground. It was during this period that the Brotherhood became internationalized, with affiliated movements springing up in Jordan, Syria, Sudan, Pakistan, Indonesia, and Malaysia. In Saudi Arabia, under the vigorous leadership of Amir (later King) Faisal ibn 'Abdul-'Aziz, the Brotherhood found refuge, and political and financial support, with funds for the Egyptian underground and salaried posts for exiled intellectuals.

## The new *jahiliya*

A radical member of the Brotherhood, Sayyid Qutb, executed in 1966 for an alleged plot to overthrow the Egyptian government, would prove to be the Sunni Muslim world's most influential Islamist theorist. Some of Qutb's key ideas, however, are directly attributable to the Indian scholar and journalist Abul Ala Maududi, whose works became available in Arabic translation during the 1950s. One of Maududi's doctrines, in particular, would have a major impact on Islamic political movements. It was the idea that the struggle for Islam was not for the restoration of an ideal past, but for a principle vital to the here and now: the vice-regency of man under God's sovereignty. The jihad was therefore not just a defensive war for the protection of the Islamic territory, or *dar al-islam*. It might be waged against governments which prevent the preaching of true Islam, for the condition of *jahiliya* (the state of ignorance before the coming of Islam) was to be found currently, in the here and now.

Qutb advocated the creation of a new elite among Muslim youth who would fight the new *jahiliya* as the Prophet had fought the old one. Like the Prophet and his Companions, this elite must choose when to withdraw from the *jahiliya* and when to seek contact with it. His ideas set the agenda for Islamic radicals throughout the Sunni Muslim world. Groups influenced by them included Shukri Mustafa, a former Muslim Brotherhood activist and leader of a group known as Takfir wa Hijra ('excommunication and emigration') who followed the early Kharijis in designating grave sinners (in this case, the government) as *kafirs* (infidels); Khalid Islambuli and 'Abd al-Salam Farraj, executed for the murder of President Anwar Sadat in October 1981; and the Hizb al-Tahrir (Liberation Party) founded in 1952 by Shaikh Taqi al-Din al-Nabahani (1910–77), a graduate of al-Azhar whose writings lay down detailed prescriptions for a restored caliphate.

## The impact of the Iranian revolution

While Qutb's writings have remained an important influence on Islamic radicals or 'Islamists' from Algeria to Pakistan, a major boost to the movement came from Iran where the Ayatollah Khomeini came to power after the collapse of the Pahlavi regime in February 1979. During the final two decades of the 20th century, the Iranian Revolution remained the inspiration for Muslim radicals or 'Islamists' from Morocco to Indonesia. Despite this universalist appeal, however, the revolution never succeeded in spreading beyond the confines of Shi'i communities and even among them its capacity to mobilize the people remained limited. During the eight-year war that followed Iraq's invasion of Iran in 1980, the Iraqi Shi'is who form about 50% of the population conspicuously failed to support their co-religionists in Iran. The revolution did spread to Shi'i communities in Lebanon, Saudi Arabia, Bahrain, Afghanistan, and Pakistan, but generally proved unable to cross the sectarian divide. The new Shi'i activism in these countries either stirred up sectarian conflicts or stimulated severe repression by Sunni governments, as in Iraq and Bahrain. In Iraq, following the US-led invasion in 2003, the Shi'a majority has now asserted itself politically under a fragile democracy. Some of the credit for this achievement in the face of the chaos caused by an inept US administration of doubtful integrity is due to Grand Ayatollah Sistani, Iraq's leading *marja*, whose *fatwas* urging people – including women – to vote represented an unequivocal commitment to democratic governance. Contrary to some predictions, the Iraqi Shi'a government was very far from being an Iranian puppet or client.

Inside Iran, the success of the revolution had rested on three factors usually absent from the Sunni world: the mixing of Shi'i and Marxist ideas among the radicalized urban youth during the 1970s; the autonomy of the Shi'i religious establishment which, unlike the Sunni '*ulama*, disposed of a considerable amount of social power as a body or 'estate'; and the eschatological expectations of popular Shi'ism surrounding the return of the Twelfth Imam.

The leading Shi'i exponent of Islam as a revolutionary ideology was 'Ali Shari'ati (d. 1977), a historian and sociologist who had been partly educated in Paris. Though without formal religious training, Shari'ati reached large numbers of youth from the traditional classes through his popular lectures at the Husainiya Irshad, an informal academy he established in Tehran. Shari'ati's teachings contain a rich mix of ideas in which theosophical speculations of mystics like Ibn 'Arabi and Mulla Sadra were blended with the insights of Marx, Sartre, Camus, and Fanon (whose friend Shari'ati was and whose books he translated into Farsi). The result was an eclectic synthesis of Islamic and leftist ideas. God was virtually identified with the People, justifying revolutionary action in the name of Islam. An outspoken critic of those members of the clergy who acquiesced in the Shah's tyranny, Shari'ati drew a distinction between the official Shi'ism of the Safavid dynasty (1501–1722) which made Shi'ism the state religion in Iran, and the 'revolutionary' commitment of such archetypical Shi'i figures as the Imams 'Ali and Hussein and Abu Dharr al-Ghifari (a Companion of the Prophet often credited with socialist principles). Shari'ati's ideas, disseminated by means of photocopies and audiotapes, provided a vital link between the student vanguard and the more conservative forces which brought down the Shah's regime. The latter were mobilized by Sayyid Ruhallah Khomeini, who had come to prominence as the leading critic of Shah Mohammed Reza Pahlavi's 'White Revolution' during the early 1960s. The Shah's agricultural and social reforms threatened the interest of the religious establishment, not least because the estates from which many of the 'ulama drew their incomes were expropriated or divided up. Exiled to Najaf in Iraq, Khomeini developed his theory of government – the Vilayet-e Faqih (jurisconsult's trusteeship) – which broke with tradition by insisting that government be entrusted directly to the religious establishment.

## The tyranny of materialism

'The Europeans worked assiduously to enable the tide of this materialistic life with its corrupting traits and its murderous germs, to overwhelm all the Islamic lands toward which their hands were outstretched. . . . They laid their plans for this social aggression in masterly fashion, invoking the aid of their political acumen and their military predominance until they had accomplished their desire. They deluded the Muslim leaders by granting them loans and entering into financial dealings with them, making all of this easy and effortless for the economy and to flood the countries with their capital, their banks, and their companies; to take over the workings of the economic machinery as they wished; and to monopolize, to the exclusion of the inhabitants, enormous profits and immense wealth. After that they were able to alter the basic principles of government, justice, and education, and to imbue political, juridical and cultural systems with their own peculiar character in even the most powerful Islamic countries. They imported their half-naked women into these regions, together with their liquors, their theatres, their dance halls, their amusements, their stories, their newspapers, their novels, their whims, their silly games, and their vices.... This being insufficient for them, they founded schools, and scientific and cultural institutes in the very heart of the Islamic domain, which cast doubt and heresy into the very souls of its sons and taught them how to demean themselves, disparage their religion and their fatherland, divest themselves of their traditions and beliefs, and to regard as sacred anything Western in the belief that only that which had a European source could serve as a model to be emulated in this life. These schools took in the sons of the upper-class alone, and became a preserve restricted to them. The sons of this class consisted of the mighty and the ruling group, and those who would shortly hold within their grasp the keys of all important matters that would concern these nations and peoples.'

Hasan al-Banna, 'Between Yesterday and Today', from *Five Tracts of Hasan al-Banna: A Selection from Majmu' at Rasail al-Imam al-Shahid Hasan al-Banna*, tr. Charles Wendell (Berkeley: University of California Press, 1979), 27–8

The legitimacy of the territorial governments established after decolonization was always open to challenge on Islamic grounds. The new national states were imposed on societies where the culture of public institutions was weak and where ties of kinship prevailed over allegiances to corporate bodies. In most Middle Eastern countries and many others beyond the Muslim heartlands, the ruling institutions fell victim to manipulation by factions based on kinship, regional, or sectarian loyalties. Even when the army took power, as the only corporate group possessing internal cohesion, the elite corps buttressing the leadership were often drawn from a particular family, sect, or tribe. In the period following decolonization, the new elites legitimized themselves by appealing to nationalist goals. Their failure to 'deliver the goods' either economically or militarily (especially in the case of the states confronting Israel, and in Pakistan, which has proved unable to recover the disputed part of Kashmir from India) led to an erosion of their popular bases and the rise of movements pledged to 'restore' Islamic forms of government after years of *jahiliya* rule.

### The modern *jahiliya*

'A truly Islamic society is not one where people call themselves "Muslims", but the Islamic law has no status, even if prayers, fasting, and pilgrimage are practised and observed. It is also not an Islamic society in which people follow their own version of Islam, contrary to what Allah and His Messenger, peace be upon him, have prescribed and explained, and call it, for example, "progressive Islam". *Jahili* society appears in various forms, all of them in defiance of Divine Guidance...

'How to initiate the revival of Islam? A vanguard must set out with this determination and then keep going, marching through the vast ocean of *jahiliya* which encompasses the entire world. During its course, this vanguard, while distancing itself somewhat aloof from this all-encompassing *jahiliya*, should also retain contacts with it. The Muslims in this vanguard must know the landmarks and the milestones on the road to this goal so that they would know the starting point as well as the nature, the responsibilities, and the ultimate purpose of this long journey. Not only this, but they ought to be aware of their position *vis-à-vis* this *jahiliya* which has struck its stakes throughout the earth. They must know when to cooperate with others and when to separate from them; what characteristics and qualities they should cultivate; and with what characteristics and qualities the *jahiliya*, immediately surrounding them, is armed; how to address the people of *jahiliya* in the language of Islam; what topics and problems to discuss with them; and where and how to obtain guidance in all these matters...I have written Milestones for this vanguard, which I consider to be a waiting reality about to be materialized.'

From Sayyid Qutb, *Milestones*, tr. of *Ma'alim fi al Tariq* by Ahmad Zaki Hammad (Indianapolis: American Trust Publications, n.d.), 9

## The appeal of Islamism

Outside Iran, however, the factors that contributed to the Islamic revolution continue to sustain the Islamist movements, accounting for the continuing popularity of their ideologies. The collapse of communism and the failure of Marxism to overcome the stigma of 'atheism' has made Islamism seem an attractive ideological weapon against regimes grown increasingly corrupt, authoritarian, and sometimes tyrannical. The rhetoric of national liberation, appropriated by monopolist ruling parties, has become discredited as those parties have failed to address fundamental economic and structural problems, and are increasingly seen to be controlled by tribal coteries or political cliques indifferent to the needs of the majority. In countries such as Egypt and Algeria, qualified successes achieved by governments in the field of education have turned against them, as graduates from state universities have found their career opportunities blocked. As centres of opposition, mosques will always enjoy a certain privileged status, and the efforts of governments to subject them to state control are usually incomplete. The mosques are not just places of worship. They provide a communications network which will always be partially independent of the state. At the same time, the new communications technologies bring the previously illiterate classes into the political process in an unprecedented way, undermining the authority of literate elites, notably the 'ulama. Dale Eickelman, an American anthropologist, attributes the politicization of Islam to mass education, on the one hand, and the decline of the 'ulama, on the other:

> No longer do young men regard a long apprenticeship as the prerequisite to legitimize religious knowledge. Increasingly the carriers of religious knowledge are those who claim a strong Islamic commitment, as is the case with many educated urban youths. Freed from traditional patterns of learning and scholarship, which have often been compromised by state control, religious knowledge is increasingly interpreted in a directly political fashion.

## Urbanization and its effects

As numerous studies have shown, migration from the countryside to the city often leads to an increase in religiosity, as a more intense and self-conscious style of religious observance compensates for the more relaxed rhythms of village life. The recently urbanized underclasses are particularly susceptible to the messages of populist preachers. At the same time, the Islamist movements earn respect and gratitude by providing a network of welfare services able to fill the gaps caused by government shortfalls. Restrictions on government spending imposed by the International Monetary Fund have tended to exacerbate housing and welfare problems by forcing cuts in social spending, leading to

the withdrawal of the state from some areas and its replacement
by Islamic welfare organizations and charitable associations. Such
voluntary organizations have found generous sources of funds in
Saudi Arabia and the Gulf. With rapid urbanization and the
growth of slums and shanty-towns, the old systems ceased to
function, as shaikhs and notables, local and party bosses, became
detached from their previous clients. The former nationalist
rhetoric, whether Nasserist or Ba'thist, was discredited. 'It is into
this vacuum of organization and power', wrote Sami Zubaida,

> that the Islamic groups have stepped to impose their authority
> and discipline. The organization they impose is not one of popular
> participation. The activists and militants remain in charge, and
> the common people, to whom they provide services against
> modest payments, are considered as subjects of ethical reform, to
> be converted to orthodox conformity and mobilised in political
> support.

Yet in the tumultuous events that brought down the military-
backed regimes in Tunisia and Egypt in early 2011, the Islamists
were conspicuously absent. Among the many slogans in Cairo's
Tahrir Square calling for an end to corruption, the Islamist
war-cry 'Islam is the solution' barely featured, leading some
observers to suggest that the movement, now passed its peak, was
being overtaken by a new generation of activists committed to
democratic, secular goals. What some people were calling the
'Facebook Revolution' was an unprecedented wave of visible
public protest led by a generation of media-savvy young people,
more aware of the outside world than their parents. They were
demanding, not a 'restoration of the Shari'a', but an end to the
system of repression, corruption, and privilege that had been the
hallmark of the authoritarian Arab regimes lying between the
Atlas Mountains and the Gulf.

It would be premature, however, to conclude from the apparent
absence of Islamists in the public protests that brought down the

regimes in Tunis and Cairo that secular forms of government would necessarily prevail. In Egypt, the Muslim Brotherhood, though slow to join the protests, stood to benefit from genuinely open elections, being better organized than the overtly secular parties. After sectarian riots in a Cairo suburb, some Christians feared that a democracy weighted towards the Muslim majority would deprive them of the protection they had received under the Mubarak dictatorship. Similar fears were apparent in Syria, where minorities including Christians and Isma'ilis had enjoyed a measure of protection and local autonomy under the minority 'Alawi regime headed by the Asad family. In Tunisia, a relatively homogenous country with a well-educated population, fault lines were emerging between the more developed and secular-minded coast and the more religious and traditional inland areas. It was feared that a victory in open elections by the Islamist al-Nahda party could lead to a new military take-over, as happened in Algeria when the Islamic Salvation Front won the first round of national elections in 1991, triggering a decade of civil conflict.

Despite the successes of the 'Facebook Revolution', the spread of democracy faces formidable challenges in the Arab world 'due to the long-standing dearth … of autonomous nongovernmental associations serving as intermediaries between the individual and the state' – a feature that may be partly attributed to the absence, noted earlier, of a Shari'a concept of legal personality. The democratic deficit is far from being limited to the Arab countries. In the 2010 Democracy Index prepared by the Economist Intelligence Unit, Indonesia, the top-scoring Muslim majority country ranks 60th, in the band of 'flawed democracies', way behind most of the Latin American and East European countries, but ahead of Malaysia (71) and Mali (79). Four others (Turkey at 89, Palestine at 93, Pakistan at 104, and Iraq at 111) are listed under 'hybrid' regimes that combine elements of democracy with military or authoritarian rule. All the rest, including the former Soviet Central Asian republics, are listed as 'authoritarian', with Saudi Arabia (160) near the bottom, a little ahead of North Korea

(167). This is not to argue that Islam is necessarily inimical to democracy, but it seems self-evident that a style of religiosity that constantly harks on the unity of God and the ultimate permanence of His laws, may find it harder to work with the grain of democracy than a pluralistic religion such as India's, with its pantheon of deities embedded in the popular culture.

13. The logo of the Lebanese Hizbullah, the 'Party of God', reflects the blend of religion and revolutionary 'agitprop' common to most Islamist movements

## The international dimension

Though Islamist movements have usually been inspired by local conditions, the international factors should not be ignored. Veterans of the Afghan war against the Soviet occupation formed the core of armed and trained Islamist groups in Algeria, Yemen, and Egypt. At the height of the Afghan war against the Soviets, there are said to have been between 10,000 and 12,000 *mujahidin* from Arab countries financed from mosques and private contributions in Saudi Arabia and the Gulf states. Many of them, ironically, are reported to have been trained by the CIA. Hardened jihadists who honed their skills fighting the Soviets were well placed to combat the US and other NATO forces after the overthrow of the Afghan Taliban regime in 2003. The persistence of the Taliban insurgency against the US-backed government in Kabul well into the second decade of the 21st century depended on a combination of factors, including Taliban control of the drugs trade, financing from wealthy sympathizers in the Gulf region, support from elements in the Pakistan military and intelligence services (who, despite official denials, had protected bin Laden for several years), and a generalized hostility to a military occupation by foreigners (the same factors that assisted the successful jihad against the Soviets).

Everywhere Islamization policies, whether imposed 'from above' by governments, or applied locally 'from below', have led to restrictions on the rights of women and religious minorities as modernist interpretations have given ground to more traditionalist attitudes. The tendency to articulate political aims in Islamic terms found constituencies in newly urbanized migrants whose understandings were typically formed in rural village *milieus* by mullahs or *'ulama* with minimal access to modernist influences. Consequently, the modernist tendency which formed an important strand in the discourse of 'Abduh, Qutb, al-Banna, and even (to a lesser extent) Maududi tends to wither before the traditionalism of the recently mobilized masses.

This has by no means happened everywhere, however. In central Asia, the people generally rejected the 'Islamist' alternative after the collapse of the Soviet Union, despite a resurgence of Islamic activity among the young and a revival of Islamic education in schools and colleges. While Russian manipulation partly accounted for the return of the old communist *nomenklaturas* under new nationalist labels, it is also clear that in societies where literacy is universal a consensus in favour of Islamic forms of government is conspicuously absent.

## The problem of modernization

In the Muslim heartlands, as Olivier Roy has pointed out, modernization has already occurred, but it has not been absorbed within a commonly recognized and accepted conceptual framework. It has happened 'through rural exodus, emigration, consumption, the change in family behaviour (a lower birthrate) but also through the cinema, music, clothing, satellite antennas, that is, through the globalization of culture'. The resulting confusion has particularly affected the position of women, formerly the protected and symbolically 'invisible' half of traditional Muslim societies. As in most other parts of the world, the global economy is breaking down old extended family structures, leading to a growing necessity for women to earn cash incomes or to increase their earnings and be recognized for their efforts. Similar considerations apply to sectarian issues. Under modern conditions, sectarian or ethnic rivalries that coexisted in a rough or ritualized manner in pre-modern times acquire a murderous dimension. In marked contrast to their predecessors, Muslim majority national or regional governments have tried to enforce legal and ideological uniformity on all their citizens, regardless of religious background. The result has been a significant increase in sectarian conflicts in countries with different Muslim traditions, including Turkey, the only fully functioning democracy in the Middle East. Inter-religious and inter-communal tensions have flared up not only in Egypt and

Malaysia but also in Sudan, Nigeria, Iran, Afghanistan, Bangladesh, and Indonesia. The resulting conflicts have varied from acts of discrimination to forms of violence, including individual assassinations and the destruction of villages, churches, schools, hospitals, and mosques.

Iraq and Pakistan have seen vicious sectarian attacks mainly directed at Shi'i worshippers, who are systematically targeted by suicide bombers. In Bahrain, democratic protests by Shi'a complaining about decades of repression under a minority Sunni regime have been brutally suppressed by their government with the aid of its Saudi co-religionists. A few hundred kilometres to the west, in the Arab republic of Syria, hundreds, possibly thousands, of protestors have been shot by security forces commanded by a Shi'a sectarian group – the so-called 'Alawis – who hold the levers of power.

## The future of Islamism

Despite its apparent absence from the stated political agenda of the 'Facebook' rebels, Islamism seems set to remain a significant political factor in Muslim lands for the foreseeable future. Yet for all the anxieties about a future 'clash of civilizations', it seems unlikely to effect significant external political change. Although radical pan-Islamists of al-Qaeda and Hizb-ul-Tahrir who yearn for a restored caliphate will continue to challenge their legitimacy, existing Muslim states are locked into the international system. The territorial state, though never formally sanctified by Islamic tradition, is proving highly resilient, not least because of the support it receives militarily and economically through the international system. Local conflicts arising from the position of Muslim majorities residing under non-Muslim governments – as in Indian-ruled Kashmir or Russian-ruled Chechnya – may take the form of 'jihads', especially when nurtured by pan-Islamist forces such as al-Qaeda. The Turkic and Tajik Muslims of western China, under pressure from Han Chinese colonization and settlement, could adopt a similar path. The emergence of real democracy in Egypt, with or without a dominant role for the Muslim Brotherhood, could place Israel under increasing pressure to abandon its system of functional apartheid and sacrifice some of its Palestinian colonies in the interests of peace. The converse – of a Muslim majority government resisting a secessionist movement backed by foreign or 'Christian' powers – could set the scenario for a renewed civil war in Sudan, where a referendum in January 2011 overwhelmingly backed independence for the oil-rich, predominantly Christian south. All such local or regional conflicts can be presented rhetorically as 'jihad' directed against the hostile infidel.

In the longer term, the globalization of culture through the revolution in communications technology must lead to a form of secularization in Muslim societies, not least because of the increasing availability of religious and cultural choice. As a community of believers without a formal priesthood, Islam may be better placed than its ancient Christian rival to take advantage of information systems that are decentralized and free from hierarchical control. As Gary Bunt, a leading authority on 'Cyber-Islam' explains, 'an innovative knowledge and proselytizing economy' is emerging, reliant on 'collaborative, horizontal knowledge' and 'peer-to peer networking', challenging the authority of traditional 'top-down' models of religious authority, taking Islam, with its multiplicity of facets and traditions, into the uncharted realms of cyberspace. Although literate Muslims with access to the internet are currently a minority, the proportion, and influence, of the believers Bunt calls 'i-Muslims' is bound to grow as the technologies and the skills required to access them spread exponentially over the coming decades.

The internet offers something new in the world – the democratization of religiosity. Although major figures such as Ayatollah Sistani and Yusuf al-Qaradawi can respond to believers' questions by issuing online *fatwas*, the very plurality of sites – plus the availability of alternative views – must challenge their authority in the long term. The proliferation of Islamic websites makes it difficult to maintain the fiction that one version of Islam – whether Sunni or Shi'i, traditionalist, 'salafist' (literalist), reformist, or modernizing – however well funded, must predominate over others. Issues considered forbidden or taboo, such as homosexuality, are freely discussed online through sites such as al-Fatiha and Queer Jihad. The exclusion of women from religious leadership, or their confinement to inferior quarters of mosques, are ventilated and discussed. Scandalous political realities, such as illegal Israeli settlements and mistreatment of Palestinians, are exposed, and challenged, by the Electronic Intifada (named after the two Palestinian rebellions). Other facts are exposed and amplified, such as the explosive US diplomatic cables revealed by Wikileaks. These included the revelation that the Saudis refer to Iran, a fellow Muslim nation, as 'evil', and that instead of pursuing its publicly stated priority of pressuring its American allies over Israel, the Saudi ruler requested them to 'cut off the head of the snake' by attacking and occupying Iran. The same cables reveal that long after Saudis expelled bin Laden and removed his citizenship, the main financiers of al-Qaeda continued to be Saudi donors.

Al-Qaeda itself, of course, has been a leading beneficiary of the web. Bunt suggests that 'without the Internet and its associated tools al-Qaeda could not have functioned as it did', communicating its various agendas, aims, and objectives while attracting would-be jihadists to its cause. Images of oppression and violence suffered by Muslims in different theatres, filmed by networks such as the Qatar-based al-Jazeera channel or circulated in amateur footage captured on YouTube, have been catalysts for radicalization. The London transport bombings in July 2005 were clearly inspired by images of the slaughter and abuse suffered by Muslims at the hands of Anglo-American forces in Iraq. As a mirror of actual realities, the internet, like the television spotlight it is coming to replace in public consciousness, has a distorting effect, given that the more developed parts of the world (Israel-Palestine, Iraq, and the industrialized North) have more access to social networking and interactive media than regions such as Darfur in the less developed South. Violence, where it occurs, makes for more dramatic viewing than the quotidian duties of ritual prayer and charity.

Generally, it may be suggested that the internet contributes to the sense of 'being Muslim' by giving people access to a 'cyber-community' of like-minded people whose identity as Muslims transcends the particularities of family, nationality, language, or ethnicity. The proliferation of websites showing the availability of potential Muslim marriage-partners suggests that arranged and cousin marriages, *de rigueur* for many families, are becoming outmoded. In that respect, the emerging 'cyber-*umma*' may have some impact on the real one, enhancing its sense of identity by reinforcing its transnational ties and social networks. At the same time, however, the cyber-revolution subverts the idea, promoted by Salafists and Islamists, that Islam is a monolith, by exposing the diversity of views and interpretations. In the new 'cyber-*umma*', every believer becomes a *mujtahid* – a qualified interpreter capable of using his or her reasons and judgement in understanding the text. Here a factor of increasing significance will be the presence of a large and growing Muslim diaspora educated in the West and able to rediscover in Islam a *voluntary* faith freed from the imperatives of enforcement, while finding an outlet for Islamic values through voluntary activity.

The Isma'ili community headed by the Aga Khan offers an impressive example of how Islamic concerns for welfare and social justice can be harnessed to the ancient structure of the Imamate on the basis of esoteric understandings of Islam, in which the two jihads, the activist and the quietist, have been fused together in a dynamic combination, and charged with creative energy. Another, more controversial, example is the Gulen movement, based in Turkey. With a membership estimated at up to 8 million in countries ranging from Kenya to Kazakhstan, Gulen is linked to more than a thousand schools in 130 countries, as well as numerous media enterprises under a flexible organizational regime that is distinctly modern while having some affinities with the old Sufi *tariqas*. While its mostly secular critics condemn it as a cult aiming to achieve political power by concealing its true objectives, its defenders insist that the version of Islam preached by its founder Fetullah Gulen, who currently resides in the United States, is both ecumenical – engaging in constructive dialogue with religionists and humanists – and enlightened, with more emphasis given to the provision of schools and scholarships than the construction of mosques. As an organization that receives tithes from its members and combines *pro bono* or charitable activities with for-profit enterprises, it bears some similarities to the Aga Khan Development Network (AKDN). However, unlike the Aga Khan, who studiously avoid engaging in political controversy, Gulen has been accused of being too close to Turkey's governing party, and journalists who have investigated his organization have found themselves in jail, after prosecutions that critics see as proof of the power that Gulen wields in the police and judiciary.

Although the political currents of exoteric Islam may still be in the ascendant, it is in the pietistic and mystical traditions that future promise lies. Both Maududi and al-Banna built pietism into their systems, believing that society must be converted before the state could be conquered. Though the militants and activists who followed them, obsessed with the corruption of governments and embittered by the appalling treatment many of them received at the hands of the police, gave priority to action, not least because killings and bombings are bound to attract attention in an international culture dominated by the media, more quietist versions of Islam may gain ground in the long term. Globalization is fast eroding the classic distinction between *dar al-islam* and *dar al-harb*. The Islamic Republic of Iran, far from being identified with the new political forces emerging in the Middle East, is more likely to be identified with the old, repressive, authoritarian political order. Despite the current turmoil, and the opportunities it affords for Islamist movements, the coming decades may yet see a retreat from direct political action and a renewed emphasis on the personal and private aspects of faith.

For all the efforts of political Islam to conquer the state on the basis of a new collectivist ideology constructed on the ruins of Marxism-Leninism and using some of its materials, the processes of historical and technological change point remorselessly towards increasing individualism and personal choice – primary agents of secularity. The Enlightenment has come to stay, and everybody is demanding its fruits in terms of the material benefits it offers. The problem of disentangling what is universally 'modern' from what is culturally specific to any one tradition (whether Islamic or Christian, Hindu, Buddhist, or Confucian), is far from simple. It has been addressed by such progressive Muslim intellectuals as Hasan Hanafi, Abdullahi An-Na'im, 'Abd al-Karim Soroush, and the late Muhammad Arkoun, among others. It is my own belief that, despite historical differences in the relations between the state and civil society, the Muslim world will develop along the lines previously travelled by the post-Christian West. For all the protestations to the contrary, the faith will be internalized, becoming private and voluntary. In an era when individuals are ever less bound by ties of kinship and increasingly exposed to urban anomie, Muslim souls are likely to find the Sufi path of inner exploration and voluntary association more rewarding than the world of politics. Sadly, a legacy of violence remains entrenched, and more blood can be expected to be shed.

# Appendix
# The five pillars of Islam

The basic religious duties of Muslims are known as the Five Pillars.

1. *Shahada*: declaration of faith according to the formula *There is no god but God. Muhammad is the Messenger of God.* To this, the Shi'i minority add: '*Ali is the Friend of God* (see Chapter 4).
2. *Salat*: worship. Sometimes translated as 'prayer', *salat* takes the form of a ritual prostration in which the precise bodily movements are as important as the accompanying mental activity. Sunni Muslims are required to perform *salat* five times daily – at dawn, noon, mid-afternoon, sunset, and evening. Worshippers must be in a state of ritual purity achieved by performing major or minor ablutions, depending on the degree of pollution brought about by bodily secretions, sexual activity, contact with animals, and so forth. *Salat* may be performed virtually anywhere, provided the worshipper faces the *qibla* – the direction of the Ka'ba in Makka. The congregational prayer is performed at noon on Fridays when all adult male members of the community are gathered. Males and females are usually separated, with women worshipping behind the men or in a screened-off section of the mosque. A sermon is usually delivered by the imam or prayer-leader. Under the Islamic government of Iran, Friday sermons delivered by religious leaders who are also major political players are often the occasions of major policy pronouncements.
3. *Zakat* – alms-giving/compulsory charity. This tax, payable once a year by all adult Muslims, is assessed at 2.5% of capital assets over and above a minimum known as the *nisab*. For example the *nisab* for stock

### The niceties of fasting

'The Fast of Ramadan becomes obligatory when thirty days of the preceding month, Sha'ban are past, or with the seeing of the new moon of Ramadan. This seeing is established with the testimony of one trustworthy witness, or as some say, two. If one witness is accepted, it is a condition that he must have the quality of veracity, and thus be neither a slave nor a woman . . . To fast, one must rigorously avoid coition, vomiting . . . or introducing any substance to the "interior of the body". Some make it a condition that there be in the body power to absorb the food or the medicine thus introduced. It does not matter if the "interior" is inside the head, or the belly, or the intestines or the bladder; all can break the fast with the introduction of a substance by sniffing or eating or injection, or through incision into the belly or the head, or the like. According to the soundest opinion, putting drops in the nose or the urethra breaks the fast. It is necessary [however] for such an introduction to be by an open passage. Thus there is no harm in oils entering the pores by absorption, or when kohl (antimony) is used, and its taste is afterward perceived in the throat. The introduction must be intended, so that if a fly or gnat or dust of the road or flour-dust entered by accident, the fast would not be broken. It would also not be broken if one swallowed saliva carelessly. But the fast is broken if saliva leaves the mouth and one brings it back into the mouth, or if one moistens a thread in one's mouth and then puts it back in one's mouth still moist, or if one swallows saliva in which a foreign substance or something unclean is mixed.'

Extract from instructions on observing the fast of Ramadan by Muhyi al-Din al-Nawawi (d. 1277), a *faqih* of the school of Shafi'i

consists of five camels, thirty cows (including oxen and buffaloes), or forty sheep or goats. *Zakat* is payable on bank deposits, precious metals, merchandise used in trade (but not personal possessions such as cars, clothing, houses, and jewellery), livestock, and crops from tilled land. The recipients should be the poor and needy. In the past, *zakat* was collected by the Muslim government and distributed according to pre-established patterns. Nowadays, giving is usually left to the believer's conscience.

4.  *Sawm*: the fast during Ramadan. The fast which takes place during daylight hours in the holy month of Ramadan, the ninth month of the lunar calendar, applies to eating, drinking, smoking, and sexual activity. The fast begins at dawn and ends at sunset. In Muslim countries such as Egypt, the breaking of the fast at sundown is an occasion for joyful celebration, with tables laid out in the streets and feasting that carries on well into the night. A pre-fast meal is usually served before dawn. Ramadan is traditionally an occasion for both family get-togethers and religious reflection. It is considered especially meritorious to recite the whole of the Quran during the sacred month. According to tradition, the Quran 'came down' on the 27 Ramadan, the 'Night of Power'.

5.  *Hajj*: pilgrimage to Makka. This intense and demanding religious obligation is required of every adult Muslim at least once in his or her lifetime. The annual pilgrimage, or *Hajj*, takes place during the last ten days of the twelfth lunar month (Dhu al-Hijja) reaching its climax with the Feast of Sacrifice ('Id al-Adha), a festival honoured throughout the Muslim world with the slaughter of a specially fattened sheep, cow, or camel in commemoration of the Sacrifice of Abraham. The minor pilgrimage, or *'Umra*, may be performed at any time of the year. In the past, Muslims from far-flung regions would spend the best part of a lifetime on the journey, working their way across Africa or Asia to reach the Holy City. On their return, they enjoyed the honoured status of *Hajji* – one who has made the pilgrimage. Nowadays, the journey has been greatly facilitated by inexpensive air transport. About two million pilgrims perform the *Hajj* annually. Half of them come from overseas. Their numbers are limited by a quota system operated by the Saudi authorities, guardians of the Holy Places in conjunction with Muslim governments. The arduous rituals, often performed in the intense heat of an Arabian summer, include the *Tawaf* – the circumambulation of the Ka'ba; the *Sa'i* (seven-fold running between the hillocks of Safa and Marwa, now covered in an air-conditioned gallery); the Standing in the Plain of 'Arafat, a few miles from Makka; the 'Onrush' through the narrow defile of Muzdalifa; the 'Stoning' of three pillars (*ramy al-jamarat*) representing the devil from the Jamarat Bridge; and the sacrifice of an animal at Mina (formerly performed in the open, nowadays conducted in hygienic abattoirs, with the pilgrims purchasing 'sheep certificates' for meat that will be frozen and distributed to poor families in various Muslim lands).

## The benefits of hunger

The Imam al-Ghazali's famous spiritual manual, 'The Revitalization of the Religious Sciences' (*Ihya 'Ulum al-Din*), offers a less legalistic view of fasting, emphasizing its spiritual and social virtues.

'Hunger has ten benefits. The first is the purification of the heart, the illumination of the natural disposition and the sharpening of one's insight. For satiety engenders stupidity and a blindness in the heart, and increases the vapours of the brain to produce a form of inebriation, so that the sources of thought are repressed and the heart finds it a burdensome thing to think and to perceive things with any rapidity ... The second benefit is softness and purity of the heart by which it is readied to attain the delight of intimate discourse with God and to be affected by His remembrance. ... The third benefit lies in mortification and abasement, and the removal of exultation, rejoicing and exuberance, which comprises the beginning of rebellion and heedlessness of God (Exalted is He!). For the soul is mortified and abased by nothing more effective than hunger, which, when it prevails, causes it to have placid trust in its Lord and fear of Him, and to be aware of its helplessness and abasement when it weakens and becomes desperate for the morsel of bread which it misses, so that the whole world appears dark to a man because one drink of water did not come when he desired it. ... The fourth benefit is that one comes never to forget God's trials and torments, or those who are afflicted by them, for the man sated is liable to forget those people who are hungry and to forget hunger itself. ... The fifth and greatest benefit lies in the breaking of all one's desires for sin, and achieving mastery over the soul which commands evil. For all sin originates in one's desires and strengths, the stuff of which is food in every case: when one eats less, every one of one's desires and strengths will be enfeebled. ... This does not constitute one single benefit; rather it is the storehouse of all benefits, for this reason it has been said that "hunger is one of God's storehouses".'

From the 'On Breaking the Two Desires': Book 23 of the *Ihya 'Ulum al-Din*, tr. T. J. Winter, Cambridge Islamic Texts Society (1995)

In recent years, Iranian pilgrims have used the *Hajj* to make political statements attacking Israel, the West, and by implication the pro-Western Saudi dynasty, much to the annoyance of the authorities and the majority of pilgrims who regard the *Hajj* as a purely religious festival. In August 1987, the Saudis reported that 402 people, of whom 275 were Iranians, had been killed in disturbances resulting from political demonstrations. In 1990, more than 1,400 pilgrims, mainly from Turkey and Indonesia, were crushed to death in a pedestrian tunnel leading out of Makka towards Mina. Despite attempts to limit the crush of pilgrims at the ritual of stoning, there have been numerous disasters in the Jamarat Bridge area (in 1994, 1998, 2001, 2003, 2004, and 2006), together costing hundreds of lives. In 1997, several hundred pilgrims, mainly from India and Pakistan, were burned to death when fire swept through the camp at Mina.

# References

All quotations from the Quran are from *The Qur'an: A New Translation* by Tarif Khalidi (London: Penguin, 2008).

## Chapter 1

European anarchists and 'propaganda of the deed': see Malise Ruthven, *A Fury for God* (London, 2002, 2003). For statements by Osama bin Laden, see Bruce Lawrence (ed.), *Messages to the World: The Statements of Osama bin Laden* (London, 2005). 'The clash of civilizations?': Samuel Huntington, *Foreign Affairs* (72: 3, 1993), 22–9; The myth of confrontation: Fred Halliday, *Islam and the Myth of Confrontation: Religion and Politics in the Middle East* (London, 1995), 6; Thomas Hegghammer, *New York Times* 24/07/2011; uncomfortable feeling: *Guardian*, 5 May 2011; historian Fred Donner: see Fred M. Donner, *Muhammad and the Believers – At the Origins of Islam* (Cambridge, MA, 2010); social imaginary: Mohammed Arkoun, *Rethinking Islam:Common Questions, Uncommon Answers* (tr. and ed. Robert D. Lee (Boulder, CO, 1994), 6–13; 'Islamic' and 'Islamicate': Marshall G. S. Hodgson, *The Venture of Islam: Conscience and History in a World Civilization* (3 vols, Chicago, 1974), i: The Classical Age of Islam, 3–99; a ruler who has no say at all: Patricia Crone and Martin Hinds, *God's Caliph: Religious Authority in the First Centures of Islam* (Cambridge, 1986), 108–9; rise of the modern political movements in Islam: Peter von Sivers, in John Esposito (ed.), *The Oxford Encyclopedia of the Modern Islamic World* (4 vols, Oxford, 1995), ii., 259–60.

## Chapter 2

Verbal ritual enclosure: Frederick Mathewson Denny, *An Introduction to Islam* (New York, 1985), 160–1. God the implied speaker: Neal Robinson, *Discovering the Quran: A Contemporary Response to a Veiled Text* (London, 2003), xx; speculative origins: Karl-Heinz Ohlig and Gerd R. Puin (eds.), *The Hidden Origins of Islam* (Amherst, NY, 2010), 17f, 125f; acceptance of Islam: Ibn Ishaq, *The Life of Muhammad: A Translation of Ishaq's 'Sirat Rasul Allah'* (tr. and ed. Alfred Guillaume, Oxford, 1955), 117; so-called *Satanic Verses*: Guillaume, ibid., 165; prosperous Jewish farms: Kitab al-Aghani, in F. E. Peters, *Muhammad and the Origins of Islam* (Albany, NY, 1994), 193; vast flood of tradition: Chirag 'Ali, in Annemarie Schimmel, *And Muhammad Is His Messenger* (Chapel Hill, NC, 1985), 30; no official doctrine concerning prophet's sinlessness: Schimmel, ibid., 48; Jami, 'A little stone', in Schimmel, ibid., 76.

## Chapter 3

*bila kaif*: I. R. Netton, *Allah Transcendent* (London, 1994), 26; orthopraxy: Julian Baldick, 'Among the Friends of God', *Times Literary Supplement* (26 Sept. 1986); remote, unknowable God: Netton, *Allah Transcendent*, 27; 'the One Reality, God': Netton, ibid., 290; 'No one expected the Hidden Imam to arrive in a Jumbo Jet!': Shariatmadari in H. M. Heikal, *The Return of the Ayatollah* (London, 1981), 177.

## Chapter 4

endless debate: Norman Anderson, *Law Reform in the Muslim World* (London, 1976), 178; 'Whatever the Muslims see as good is good with God', George F. Hourani, *Islamic Law and Legal Theory* (ed. Ian Edge, Dartmouth, 1996), 161; Prophet's meeting with Mu'adh ibn Jabal: M. Bertrand in *Encyclopedia of Islam*, v. 281; *Ijtihad*: Sayf-al-Din al-Amidi in Edge, *Islamic Law and Legal Theory*, 281; 'from murder to social etiquette': J. N. D. Anderson, ibid., 88; judge's acute sense of observation: Lawrence Rosen, *The Anthropology of Justice Law as Culture in Islamic Society* (Cambridge 1989), 52; lack of organizational progress: Timur Kuran, *The Long Divergence: How Islamic Law Held Back the Middle East* (Princeton, 2011), 182.

## Chapter 5

*daraba*: cited by Leila Ahmed, *A Quiet Revolution* (New Haven, 2011),
266–7; sleeping foetus: Leila Badawi in Jean Holm and John
Bowker (eds.), *Women in Religion* (London, 1994), 94;
encouragement to marry: Yusuf al-Qaradawi, *The Lawful and the
Prohibited in Islam (al-halal wal-haram fil islam)* (tr. Kamal
El-Helbawy, M. Moinuddin Siddiqui, and Syed Shukry,
Indianapolis, 1985), 173; marriage and patterns of dominance:
Fuad I. Khuri, *Imams and Emirs: State, Religion and Sects in
Islam* (London, 1990), 85–8; temporary marriage: Shahla Haeri,
*Oxford Encyclopedia of the Modern Islamic World*, iv. 212; lyrical
view of life/infinite orgasm: Abdulwahab Bouhdiba, *Sexuality in
Islam* (tr. Alan Sheridan, London, 1985), ch. 7; homosexuality:
Yusuf al-Qaradawi, *The Lawful and the Prohibited in Islam*, 169;
beards: ibid. 94; the presence of females: Edward Lane, *An
Account of the Manners and Customs of the Modern Egyptians*
(London, 1836; facsimile New York, 1973), 82; Christianity and
marriage: Jack Goody, *The Development of the Family and
Marriage in Europe* (Cambridge, 1983); family sanctuaries:
E. W. Fernea in *Oxford Encyclopedia of the Modern Islamic World*,
ii. 49; Lurish hats: Freya Stark, *Letters*, ii: *The Open Door 1930–35*
(1975), 54; pupil from Grenoble: Gilles Kepel, *Allah in the West*
(Oxford, 1997), 226; half of religion received from a woman:
Soraya al-Torki in *Oxford Encylopedia of the Modern Islamic
World*, iv. 328; remythologization of society: Andrew Rippin,
*Muslims: Their Religious Beliefs and Practices*, ii: *The
Contemporary Period* (London, 1993), 124.

## Chapter 6

'To like and appreciate the customs of the infidels is a great sin':
Thanawi, in Philip Lewis, *Islamic Britain* (London, 1994), 36;
reformed Islam: Earl of Cromer, *Modern Egypt* (London, 1908),
ii. 184, 233; fatwa, 11 Nov. 1914: Rudolph Peters, *Islam and
Colonialism: The Doctrine of Jihad in Modern History* (The
Hague, 1979), 90 ff.; politicization of Islam: Dale Eickelman, in
*Oxford Encyclopedia of the Modern Islamic World*, iii. 342.

References

# Further reading

## Chapter 1

INTRODUCTORY TEXTS: Frederick Mathewson Denny, *An Introduction to Islam* (New York, 1985); Tilman Nagel, *The History of Islamic Theology*, tr. T. Thornton (Princeton, 2000); Andrew Rippin, *Muslims: Their Religious Beliefs and Practices*, i: *The Formative Period* (London, 1990), ii: *The Contemporary Period* (London, 1993); Neal Robinson, *Islam: A Concise Introduction* (London, 1999); Malise Ruthven, *Islam in the World*, 3rd edn. (London/New York, 2006); David Waines, *An Introduction to Islam* (Cambridge, 1995).

HISTORIES: Marshall G. S. Hodgson, *The Venture of Islam: Conscience and History in a World Civilization*, 3 vols. (Chicago, 1974); Albert Hourani, *A History of the Arab Peoples*, revised edn. with an Afterward by Malise Ruthven (London/Cambridge, MA, 2003); Ira Lapidus, *A History of the Islamic Peoples* (London, 1991); Chase F. Robinson et al. (eds.), *New Cambridge History of Islam*, 6 vols (Cambridge, 2010); Adam Silverstein, *Islamic History: A Very Short Introduction* (Oxford, 2009).

ENCYCLOPEDIAS/DICTONARIES: *The Encyclopedia of Islam*, rev. edn., 11 vols (Leiden, 1961–2004); John Esposito (ed.), *The Oxford Encyclopedia of the Islamic World*, 6 vols (Oxford, 2009); Lindsay Jones (ed.), *The Encyclopedia of Religion* (Detroit, 2005), vol. 7, pp. 4560–724; Richard C. Martin (ed.), *Encyclopedia of Islam and the Muslim World*, 2 vols (New York, 2004); Azim Nanji, *The Penguin Dictionary of Islam* (London, 2008); Ian Netton, *A Popular Dictionary of Islam* (London, 1997).

ATLAS: Malise Ruthven, with Azim Nanji, *Historical Atlas of the Islamic World* (Oxford, 2004).

## Chapter 2

QURAN TEXT AND COMMENTARIES IN ENGLISH: M. A. S. Abdel Haleem, *The Qur'an: A New Translation* (Oxford, 2004); Abdullah Yusuf Ali, *The Holy Qur'an: Translation and Commentary* (Lahore, 1934–7); A. J. Arberry, *The Koran Interpreted*, 2 vols (Oxford, 1964); Muhammad Asad, *The Message of the Qur'an* – with author's commentary (Gibraltar, 1980); Tarif Khalidi, *The Qur'an: A New Translation* (London, 2008) – this is the version used in this book. Numerous versions are accessible online with search facilities. Neal Robinson, *Discovering the Quran: A Contemporary Response to a Veiled Text* (London, 2003); Ziauddin Sardar, *Reading the Qur'an* (London, 2011); Michael Sells, *Approaching the Qur'an – The Early Revelations* (Ashland, OR, 2007).

ENCYCLOPEDIA: *Encyclopaedia of the Qur'an*, ed. Jane Dammen McAuliffe et al., 6 vols (Leiden, 2001–6).

BIOGRAPHIES OF MUHAMMAD: Michael Cook, *Muhammad* (Oxford, 1983); Fred McGraw Donner, *Muhammad and the Believers* (Cambridge, MA, 2010); Alfred Guillaume, *The Life of Muhammad*, tr. of Ibn Ishaq's biography (Oxford, 1987); F. E. Peters, *Muhammad and the Origins of Islam* (Albany, 1994); Barnaby Rogerson, *The Prophet Muhammad* (London, 2003). W. Montgomery Watt, *Muhammad at Mecca* (Oxford, 1953) and *Muhammad at Medina* (Oxford, 1956); condensed version: *Muhammad Prophet and Statesman* (London, 1964).

HADITH: Bukhari online with search facility: University of Southern California, http://www.usc.edu/dept/MSA/fundamentals/.../ bukhari/; *Sahih al-Bukhari*, tr. Muhammad Muhsin Khan, 9 vols (Chicago, 1979): Malik ibn Anas, *Al-Muwatta*, tr. Aisha Abdurrahman al-Tarjumana and Yacoub Johnson (Norwich, 1982); Muslim ibn Hajjaj al-Qushayri, *Al-Jami sl-Sahih*, tr. William Chittick (Albany, NY, 1981).

HADITH CRITICISM: Daniel W. Brown, *Rethinking Tradition in Modern Islamic Thought* (Cambridge, 1996); Ignaz Goldziher, *Muslim Studies*, tr. and ed. S. M. Stern (London, 1971); Joseph Schacht, *The Origins of Muhammadan Jurisprudence* (Oxford, 1950).

## Chapter 3

Abbas Amanat, *Apocalyptic Islam and Iranian Shi'ism* (London, 2009); Hamid Dabashi, *Shi'ism – A Religion of Protest* (London and Cambridge, MA, 2011); Farhad Daftary, *The Isma'ilis: Their History and Doctrines* (Cambridge, 2007), and *A Short History of the Ismailis* (Edinburgh, 1998); Asghar Ali Engineer, *The Bohras* (New Delhi, 1980); Heinz Halm, *Shiism* (Edinburgh, 1991); Wilferd Madelung, *The Succession to the Prophet* (Cambridge, 1996); Moojen Momen, *An Introduction to Shi'i Islam* (New Haven, 1985); Matti Moosa, *Extremist Shiites – The Ghulat Sects* (Syracuse, 1988); Seyyed Vali Nasr, *The Shia Revival: How Conflicts within Islam Will Shape the Future* (New York, 2006); Yann Richard, *Shi'ite Islam*, tr. Antonia Nevill (Oxford, 1995); Barnaby Rogerson, *The Heirs of the Prophet Muhammad and the Roots of the Sunni-Shia Schism* (London, 2006).

## Chapter 4

Further reading

J. N. D. Anderson, *Law Reform in the Muslim World* (London, 1976); Norman Calder, *Studies in Early Muslim Jurisprudence* (Oxford, 1993); N. J. Coulson, *A History of Islamic Law* (Edinburgh, 1964); Ian Edge (ed.), *Islamic Law and Legal Theory* (Aldershot, 1996); Wael B. Hallaq, *A History of Islamic Legal Theories* (Cambridge, 1997); Timur Kuran, *The Long Divergence: How Islamic Law Held Back the Middle East* (Princeton, 2011); Chibli Mallat, *The Renewal of Islamic Law* (Cambridge, 1993); Abdullahi Ahmed An-Na'im, *Islam and the Secular State: Negotiating the Future of Shari'a* (Cambridge, MA, 2008); Lawrence Rosen, *The Anthropology of Justice – Law as Culture in Islamic Society* (Cambridge, 1989); Joseph Schacht, *An Introduction to Islamic Law* (Oxford, 1964).

## Chapter 5

Janet Afary, *Sexual Politics in Modern Iran* (Cambridge, 2009); Leila Ahmed, *Women and Gender in Islam: Historical Roots of a Modern Debate* (New Haven, 1992), and *A Quiet Revolution: The Veil's Resurgence from the Middle East to America* (New Haven, 2011); Lois Beck and Nikki R. Keddie (eds.), *Women in the Muslim World* (Cambridge, MA, 1978); Abdalwahab Bouhdiba, *Sexuality in Islam*, tr. Alan Sheridan (London, 1985); Deniz Kandiyoti (ed.), *Women, Islam and the State* (Philadelphia, 1991); Fatima Mernissi, *Beyond the Veil: Male-Female Dynamics in Modern Muslim Society* (London, 1985); *Women and Islam: An Historical and Theological Inquiry*, tr. Mary Jo Lakeland (Oxford, 1991); Joan Wallach Scott, *The Politics of the Veil* (Princeton, 2007); Sherifa Zuhur, *Revealing Reveiling: Islamist Gender Ideology in Contemporary Egypt* (Albany, NY, 1992).

## Chapter 6

SUFISM: Julian Baldick, *Mystical Islam: An Introducton to Sufism* (London, 1989); Carl W. Ernst (tr.), *Teachings of Sufism* (Boston, 1999); Michael Sells (tr.), *Early Islamic Mysticism* (New York, 1996); Annemarie Schimmel, *Mystical Dimensions of Islam* (Chapel Hill, NC, 1975).

ISLAMIC REFORM, POLITICAL ISLAM, MODERN TRENDS, AND MILITANCY: Aziz al-Azmeh, *Islams and Modernities* (London, 1993); Gary Bunt, *Virtually Islamic: Computer-Mediated Communication and Cyber Islamic Environments* (Cardiff, 2000); John Calvert, *Sayyid Qutb and the Origins of Radical Islamism* (London, 2010); Dale F. Eickelman and James Piscatori, *Muslim Politics* (Princeton, 1996); Roger Hardy, *The Muslim Revolt – A Journey Through Political Islam* (London, 2010); Gilles Kepel, *Muslim Extremism in Egypt* (Berkeley, 1993), and *The War for Muslim Minds: Islam and the West* (Cambridge, MA, 2004); Jytte Klausen, *The Islamic Challenge: Politics and Religion in Western Europe* (Oxford, 2005), and *The Cartoons that Shook the World* (New Haven, 2009); Gudrun Krämer, *Hasan al-Banna* (London, 2010); Pervez Hoodbhoy, *Islam and Science: Religious Orthodoxy and the Battle for Rationality* (Kuala Lumpur, 1992); Albert Hourani, *Arabic Thought in the Liberal Age* (Cambridge, 1983); Yusuf al-Qaradawi, *The Lawful and the Prohibited in Islam*, tr. L. el-Helbawy et al. (Indianapolis, *c.* 1960); Olivier Roy, *Globalised Islam: The Search for a New Umma* (London, 2004); Malise Ruthven, *A Fury for God: The Islamist Attack on America* (London, 2002) and *Encounters with Islam* (London, 2012); Amyn Sajoo, *Muslim Modernities: Expressions of the Civil Imagination* (London, 2008); Suha Taji-Farouki and Basheer M. Nafi (eds.), *Islamic Thought in the Twentieth Century* (London, 2004).

# Index

Index

# Expand your collection of
# VERY SHORT INTRODUCTIONS